Activities
That Teach

Activities That Teach

by Tom Jackson M.Ed.

Red Rock Publishing

Credits
Cover Design: Bill Kuhre, Kuhre Ad Art
Page Design and Typesetting: Accu-Type Typographers
Printing: Publisher's Press

First Printing 1993
Second Printing 1994
Third Printing 1995
Fourth Printing 1996
Fifth Printing 1997
Sixth Printing 1998
Seventh Printing 1999
Eighth Printing 2000
Ninth Printing 2001

Library of Congress Cataloging-in-Publication Data
Jackson, Tom
    Activities That Teach
    Card number 93-16169

ISBN 0-9664633-1-5

Additional copies of this book may be ordered from your book supplier or from:
Active Learning Center, Inc.
3835 West 800 North
Cedar City UT 84720
(435) 586-7058 between the hours of 7:00 a.m. and 7:00 p.m. Mountain Time
Fax: (435) 586-0185
Toll free: 1-888-588-7078 between the hours of 7:00 a.m. and 7:00 p.m.
    Mountain Time

Web Site: www.activelearning.org

Have Tom Jackson speak to your organization or conference. Call for information.

Printed in the United States of America

CONTENTS

Chapter One: 1
What is Active Learning?

Chapter Two: 7
Importance of Active Learning

Chapter Three: 13
Why Use Active Learning?

Chapter Four: 19
**Overcoming Objections to
    Active Learning**

Chapter Five: 27
**Conducting an Active Learning
    Lesson**

Chapter Six: 33
Discussion: The How and The Why

Chapter Seven: 43
Discussion Formats

Chapter Eight: 49
**Using the Active Learning
    Lesson Plans**

Chapter Nine: 55
Active Learning Lesson Plans

A Million Dollars 56
    Drugs, Values

All Thumbs 59
    Alcohol, Other Drugs

All Tied Up 62
    Addiction, Habits

Auction Block 64
    Goal Setting, Values

Awesome Lap Sit 70
    Communication, Problem Solving

Back Art 73
    Communication

Back to Back Drawing 76
    Communication

Bad Vision 80
    Alcohol

Balloon Race 82
    Alcohol, Other Drugs

Blind Line Up 85
    Communication

Blind Walk 87
    Communication

Body Shuffle 90
    Communication, Decision Making,
      Problem Solving

Bridges 93
    Decision Making, Problem Solving

Building What You Hear 96
    Communication

Choices and Consequences 100
    Decision Making

Cilia Volleyball 103
Tobacco

Circle Juggle 106
Alcohol, Other Drugs, Stress

Circle Juggle With A Goal 110
Goal Setting

Connections 114
Alcohol, Other Drugs

Copy Cat 117
Goal Setting

Decide Early 119
Peer Pressure

Dollar Bill Jump 122
Alcohol, Other Drugs

Four On A String 124
Communication

Frogman 127
Addiction

Gorilla Game 129
Peer Pressure

Group Sculpture 132
Alcohol, Communication, Decision
Making, Other Drugs

Group Treasure Hunt 135
Self Esteem

How Bad Can You Be? 139
Communication

How Does It Feel? 141
Cliques, Values

I'll Bet You Can't 144
Goal Setting, Peer Pressure

In The Driver's Seat 146
Addiction, Alcohol, Other Drugs

Jogging In Place 149
Tobacco

Left Out 151
Cliques

Lights - Camera - Action 153
Advertising

Line Up 156
Self Esteem

Liver Overload 158
Alcohol

Magic Cup 160
Peer Pressure

Marshmallow Tower 162
Decision Making, Problem Solving

Mind Power 164
Goal Setting

Mount Everest 167
Decision Making, Problem Solving

Pass Right - Pass Left 170
Communication

People Jump 174
Decision Making, Problem Solving

People Lift 177
   Goal Setting

Porthole 180
   Decision Making, Problem Solving

Pressure Point 185
   Peer Pressure

Quick Draw 188
   Communication, Values

Quiet Line Up 191
   Communication

Slowed Reactions 193
   Alcohol, Other Drugs

Speed 196
   Drugs

Spin and Perform 198
   Alcohol

Squeeze 200
   Tobacco, Other Drugs

Straight Walking 203
   Alcohol

Stress Test 205
   Stress

Telegraph 207
   Communication

The Push Is On 210
   Peer Pressure, Values

Thread The Needle 213
   Alcohol, Other Drugs

Trust Circle 215
  Problem Solving, Self Esteem

Unknown 218
  Drugs

Vanishing Circle 221
  Goal Setting

Whose Fault Is It? 223
  Decision Making, Peer Pressure

Bibliography and Resource List..................... 229

Topical Index 233

ACKNOWLEDGEMENTS

Anytime you work on a difficult project, such as a book, there are many people who have helped out along the way. I wish to express thanks to everyone that had a hand in the creation of this book. Bill and Minola, my parents, have to get first credit because they gave me the solid foundation that I needed to pursue my goals. Janet, my wife, has always encouraged me during our nineteen years of marriage to follow my dreams. She has been there during the trial and error years of these activities, giving advice, feedback and helping to facilitate the activities. Frank, Brent and Denise, my three children, were all used as guinea pigs for the lesson plans. They tried out the activities before I ever took them to a classroom and helped me know when one needed changing. Frank was also my ever-patient computer teacher and helped me learn how to use a computer at the same time I wrote this book. Neal Smith has been my mentor in the field of Prevention/Education. His guidance has been invaluable to me. Many people contributed ideas to this book. Some special individuals are Tammy Hopkins, Judy Humiston, Susan Griffiths, Nikki Lovell, Verne Larsen, Doug Wiese, John Jackson and Mike Cottam. They were always willing to share their experiences and bounce ideas back and forth. I owe them and others a great big thank you. Appreciation also goes to the hundreds of kids who helped by participating in various Active Learning activities. Finally, I offer thanks to God who has strengthened me throughout my life and has given me a wonderful family to share my life with.

Chapter One

What Is Active Learning?

"For most students academic learning is too abstract. They need to see, touch and smell what they read and write about."

John I. Goodlad

For the past twenty years I have been a part of the educational system in the United States. For twelve years I was a public school teacher and for the last eight years a Prevention Specialist working with youth issues such as alcohol, drugs, tobacco, sexuality, depression, family conflicts, runaways, suicide, etc. I have seen thousands of kids in hundreds of classrooms across the country. I have determined that the system knows how to transfer facts from teacher to student, but I have also noticed that in the more abstract life skills we fall short. Life skills such as communication, problem solving, decision making, interpersonal relationships, values formation and healthy lifestyle choices are being presented in such technical formats that our students are turning a deaf ear.

I believed very early in my educational career that we needed to help our kids in these areas if they were to succeed in society. To do this effectively, I found myself frequently using non-traditional approaches. The traditional lecture, worksheet, review and test format was not impacting behavior the way I wanted. Research has shown that teachers do about 80% of the talking in most classrooms; no wonder it is said that if you want to really know something, you should teach it. I however, wanted my students to have to think for themselves and draw conclusions that were from their own thought processes, not from mine. It was after reading Edgar Dale's research concerning learning and retention that I really started researching and formalizing my approach to teaching beyond the three R's. The result was creating, collecting, adapting and refining a number of lesson plans that would impact kids. This search led me to Active Learning.

Active Learning is a concept rather than a true educational model. It combines a number of different models within it and jumps back and forth between them with great ease. Active Learning has people participate in their own learning process by involving them in some type of activity where they physically become a part of the lesson. Examples of this would be role-playing, simulations, debates, demonstrations, problem solving initiatives, skits, video productions, discussions, games, etc. Two teaching strategies that fit into this concept are Cooperative Learning and Experiential Learning. Both of these involve the learner as an active participant in the educational process.

Active Learning is based on a process rather than an outcome. What is learned as the activity takes place is as important as any of the facts that are an outcome of the activity. It is the interaction among the students that bring this learning about. Patricia and Timothy Greene wrote in their book, *Substance Abuse Prevention Activities for Secondary Students,* "An important fact about the process approach is that the skills that are taught are transferable to other tasks. Process skills are not isolated bits of knowledge, but broad skills that can be used for a lifetime." Active Learning is an effective tool to teach not only information, but lifelong living skills. Through the process, an individual can internalize information and assume responsibility for their decisions regarding personal lifestyle choices.

Active Learning has some aspects of left and right brain research in it. The approach to lesson plans is definitely set up that way. The first part of the lesson is logical and feeds the left brain with an introduction of facts, thereby giving the students some basic knowledge to work with. The second part of the lesson is very right brain: You reinforce that knowledge and allow for an understanding of it's importance by involving them in an activity. Many people assume that fun and learning can't occur at the same time. This is simply not true. By using an approach that utilizes fun, learning is not automatically eliminated. Some people equate a quiet classroom or a well behaved student with learning, but observations are showing us that kids may just be day dreaming while you are talking or memorizing answers to test questions without any real impact being made on their way of thinking.

The right side of the brain involves more of the emotional faculties of the brain. The physical movement and varied assault on the body's senses helps to imprint the activity on the student's brain. After completion of the activity, you shift back again to the more logical left side of the brain. The process that took place during the activity is reinforced through a debriefing or discussion time. The students talk about what took place and the importance of the interactions. The whys and the hows can be explored during this time. Then the students discuss how the activity can be applied to their lives. It is during this discussion time that the students can transfer what they learned from the activity to their own lifestyle.

Let me caution those of you who are thinking, "This sounds neat but I can't do it in my class." I do not advocate the use of Active Learning as the only teaching technique that you use in your class. It is but one of the tools that you can have at your disposal. Used properly, Active Learning can help you in a variety of ways to teach information that is difficult to transmit via other formats. I agree that if used exclusively this or any other method of teaching would lose it's appeal and effectiveness. I also caution you however, not to discard this technique just because it is different from what you have been using or because it sounds like too much fun.

Active Learning Process

1. **General concept is presented to the group.**

2. **Specific information concerning the concept is received by the group.**

3. **Activity is undertaken by the group.**

4. **Group explores actions and consequences during the activity.**

5. **Group discussion is held immediately following the conclusion of the activity.**

6. **General principles are discussed.**

7. **Specific life applications are derived from the general principles.**

8. **Life applications are internalized by individuals according to their needs and readiness.**

9. **Students act on what they have learned.**

While this is Active Learning at its best, you must realize that Active Learning is like an adventure. You can not predict exactly what will happen. What you can be sure of is this: Whatever learning does take place will be significant to those involved; they will own what they learn and will retain that knowledge for a longer period of time than through any method of passive learning that we have discovered yet. It is the process that makes Active Learning the teaching tool that it is, and this process has a synergistic quality about it, meaning what comes out is greater than what goes in. I hope you enjoy watching your students explore the world of decisions, consequences, emotions and opinions through the use of Active Learning.

Chapter Two

Importance of Active Learning

"The only learning that really sticks is that which is self discovered."

Carl Rodgers

A great deal of research has been done into the way people learn. One fact keeps repeating itself over and over again and that is people who are involved in their own learning process will understand more and remember the information to which they were exposed for a longer period of time. Howard Hendricks in his book *Teaching To Change Lives,* stated it this way, "Maximum learning is always the result of maximum involvement." It is involvement that seems to be the key. Active Learning allows people to become involved in their education. This involvement can occur through role playing, simulations, games, discussions, demonstrations and problem solving initiatives. In the book *Creative Teaching Methods,* Marlene LeFever puts it this way, "Participation in the learning process stimulates learning and encourages growth. When children and adults participate in the learning process, truth becomes real in their lives." We talk about teaching values and attitudes, but few teaching techniques allow us to really affect the inner mind of people. This is one of the important factors of Active Learning. It is a teaching method which allows students to transfer facts into behavior.

People do not succeed by facts alone. The education system has recognized this fact for some time now and has been active in teaching life skills, living skills and social skills for the past several years. Active Learning uses many approaches to address these skill areas and apply that knowledge to the lives of individuals. It's effectiveness is recognized in *Games for Social and Life Skills* by Tim Bond. He states, "... games offer the participants structured experiences that are particularly suitable for improving social skills. The structure of the game can focus the experience on specific issues. In addition, learning by direct personal experience has far more impact than being advised on the basis of someone else's experience, which is inevitably second hand. First hand experience makes it easier for someone to relate to whatever they have learned from the game and apply it to everyday life." Another author, Spencer Kagan, in his book *Cooperative Learning* points out the benefits of participatory learning in the area of self esteem. He states, "Almost all studies which compare the self esteem of students following cooperative and traditional interaction, show significant gains favoring students in cooperative classrooms."

Helping kids to succeed after graduation means giving them the skills necessary to communicate and interact with others. John D. Rockefeller was quoted as saying,

"I will pay more for the ability to deal with people than any other ability under the sun." This thought is reinforced by one survey which determined that the most common reason people are fired from their first job is not what they know, but rather their inability to relate with others on the job. Even with this knowledge, traditional teaching methods consistently emphasize information at the expense of interpersonal skills. David Johnson, in his book *Cooperation In The Classroom,* states, "grades in school do not predict which students will have a high quality of life after they graduate. The ability to work with others does." Active Learning can provide a vehicle for the teaching of these interpersonal skills while still covering material that is basic in any educational system. These interpersonal skills are not only important in the work place, but in all areas of our lives, whether it be our job, family, community or other relationships. This teaching technique allows a variety of ways to foster communication skills, higher-level thinking skills and social skills. These are skills which are in demand no matter what area of life you wish to discuss. No longer can we sit back and give book knowledge without rounding out the educational process with skills that allow our graduates to participate in our increasingly complicated and interdependent society. These skills are not easily taught nor easily learned. This difficulty is exactly why the use of Active Learning is important. It allows the student to practice these skills while in the safe confines of a classroom and with the guiding hand of a teacher.

Advantages of Active Learning

1. **Students are motivated.** The approach has a certain amount of fun included in it. Fun is a motivating

factor for kids. It is easier to teach kids when they think they are enjoying themselves, even if the fun involves learning. Just by doing something that is a little different, kids become motivated to participate.

2. **Takes place in a safe environment.** The classroom is a place where experimentation and failure should not only be allowed, but encouraged. Without risks being taken, real learning comes to a halt. The teacher can provide that safe environment through modeling and setting acceptable limits of behavior in the classroom. This would include ruling out name calling, singling out individuals for ridicule, sarcasm, and other degrading behaviors.

3. **Participation by the entire group.** Being actively involved means that the students are part of the lesson plan. Information is not given to them; they go after it. This is a "get up and go" type of learning that places everyone in a position to benefit from being a part. Some activities require strength; other activities require brains, and still other activities simply require a person to be a participant. Everyone finds a place and contributes in his own way.

4. **Each person takes responsibility for his own learning.** As a participant in the Active Learning process, the students must make their own assumptions and decisions about what is taking place. Others can tell them what to think, but each person is responsible for deciding if that reasoning is right for him. This is the challenge of an Active Learning model. No one has the right or wrong answer, each person can interpret the action for himself and apply it to his own circumstance.

5. **It is flexible and thereby relevant.** The same activities can be used with a wide range of age groups. Some of the rules or language may have to be changed when sliding up and down the grade levels, but the basic activity can remain essentially the same. By making changes you can make an activity relevant to a wide variety of age groups while still exploring the same concepts. Age or developmental appropriateness is easily accomplished through variations and adaptations which can be made by the teacher.

6. **Receptiveness is increased.** Many topics when approached through traditional teaching models are automatically tuned out by kids because they feel "preached to." By using an Active Learning approach where the principles and application of those principles are expressed by the kids themselves, the information becomes easier for them to hear and apply.

7. **Inductive reasoning is stimulated.** Answers are not given, but rather explored. Questions must be asked and answered before the activity can be completed. Many of the questions and answers come from the students themselves during the course of the activity. Kids will use trial and error to move through many of the activities. It will be during this discussion of ideas and the subsequent processing, that much of the learning will take place.

8. **Participants reveal their thought processes.** While the activity is taking place and during the discussion after the activity, the teacher is able to determine the level of student understanding. He can now concentrate his teaching on the areas of

greatest need. The key is to listen to what the students are saying. Their words are a window into their minds. Too many of our teaching techniques emphasize the instructor doing so much talking that he never gets to hear what the students are thinking other than the required responses during question and answer time; Active Learning allows you to hear them as they think, decide, act and process different situations that you place them in.

9. **Allows for the correction of failure.** In real life when we make a mistake it is hard to go back and replay the tape of life and correct it. In an activity format, if you make a mistake that results in failure you can stop the activity, discuss other options and start over again. Barriers and dead ends become "teaching moments" where the class learns that mistakes can be beneficial and lead to something better, rather than failure being the end of trying.

10. **Allows for greater risk taking.** Kids feel free to participate and learn through involvement because they know the activity is not real. Taking risks is hard in a society that idolizes winners and throws away losers. When we see an Olympic athlete who has finished second being asked why he didn't get the gold, you know that society feels winning is everything. By allowing students to participate without the stress of having to win, you give them the freedom to try without the disgrace of failure.

Chapter Three

Why Use Active Learning?

"Knowledge cannot be passed like a material substance from one mind to another; for thoughts are not objects which may be held and handled . . . Ideas must be reexperienced."
John Milton Gregory

Much of the teaching that we do today is outcome based; we are looking for the learner to acquire a certain set of facts or body of knowledge. This has manifested itself in the significant growth of multiple choice testing, which is being used almost exclusively in many classrooms. While this type of testing has a place in education, it needs to be balanced by teaching students that the process by which they arrive at answers can be as important for their future success as the answers themselves. Some people are asking the question, "Which is more important, to have students learn the outcomes of previous reasoning or to have students learn the skills to conduct their own research?" I feel that both strategies have their usefulness, but we have placed too much emphasis on the former and not enough on the latter. In the book *Cooperative Learning* by Spencer Kagan, he states "Exclusive study of the products of prior work looks back, disempowering students, conducting creative investigations looks forward, empowering students." It is this empowerment of the student that we wish to encourage through Active Learning.

If we want learning and problem solving to be a continual and lifelong process which will result in changes of attitude, values and beliefs, then we need to emphasize process over content. We are an information society. Presently the rate of new information, especially in the scientific and technical fields, doubles every two years according to Elizabeth Christopher in her book *Leadership Training Through Gaming*. She also concludes that this rate will continue through the end of the century.

When we lock our students into memorizing strictly content or understanding hypothesis developed by others, we have relegated them to proving the past but not developing the future. Active Learning through such exercises as role playing, simulations, initiative problems, games, demonstrations, and discussions provides a great opportunity to teach process. Active Learning allows people to learn from the inside out in a four step process. The first step involves experiencing feelings during the activity. The second step is to use inductive reasoning to work through the activity and complete it. The third step involves discussing what happened during the activity, and the fourth step is to apply what was experienced and observed during the activity to general and personal situations.

Active Learning is a technique which allows students to become more directly involved in their education. In their book *Do It! Active Learning In Youth Ministry* by Thom and Joani Schultz, they state that "Studies reveal that the more students become involved in an experience, the more they'll learn from it." In addition, research has shown that kids are more motivated to learn when they are active participants in their own learning process. Part of this learning factor is in the format of Active Learning itself; students are able to get immediate feedback during the activity from others involved in the same activity. With teacher guidance, peers are teaching peers to solve problems and overcome artificially created barriers. As an added plus, the students find Active Learning to be a fun way to learn. This increases their willingness to be involved and some learn in spite of themselves.

Retention is a key component of learning. If you take a look at professor of education Edgar Dale and his "Cone Of Learning" research on retention, you will find some teaching techniques which produce a higher percentage of retention. His research at Ohio State University measured the degree of effectiveness each teaching technique had on retention. He found that students will remember five to fifteen percent of what they read or hear, ten to twenty percent of what they see, and forty to fifty percent if the information is presented both visually and verbally. A good example of this would be television programs or movies. We receive input both verbally and visually in both of these mediums. People will be able to describe to you scene by scene what they experienced at the movie theater for weeks after attending. If discussion is the teaching technique, then students will remember up to sixty to seventy percent of what was discussed. However, the highest retention rate (up to ninety percent) involves personal experience. Active Learning combines all of the aforementioned teaching techniques: Students hear information; they see the activity take place; they are involved in a follow-up discussion, and in most cases, they personally experience what takes place.

Active Learning also addresses the needs of different types of learners. A lot of research has been done on the different ways that people learn. Every class or group will have a number of each type of learner. The main groups of learners are visual, auditory and kinesthetic. Each group is classified by which sensory stimuli they prefer when acquiring new information. Each classification classifies which type of stimuli is preferred and most effective for that particular group. Visual learners perform best when they can see new information as it is presented to them. Auditory learners absorb information through the spoken word. Most teachers fall into this category; they enjoyed school and found it to be a pleasant experience since most of the teaching done in today's school system is through auditory techniques. Because of this pleasant experience, they chose teaching as their profession. Kinesthetic learners are those that learn through touch or movement. Kinesthetic learners are most often male and many times, lower achieving students. The low achievement logically follows, as physical involvement is the least used technique in our schools. This group makes up about twenty-five percent of the student population, yet the most effective teaching technique is almost totally ignored except in such classes as shop and physical education. Active Learning allows all three groups to use their particular talent in the learning process. Rather than favoring one group over another, it combines all three. This is why the technique is so successful, even with high risk students.

Teachers can use Active Learning for a number of outcomes. David Johnson, in his book *Cooperation In The Classroom*, states that this type of learning "should be used when we want students to learn more, like school better, like each other better, like themselves better and learn more effective social skills." I think that any teacher would want to see these outcomes in their students. Active Learning can be used to confirm, modify or refute prior beliefs. It gives the teacher a perfect vehicle to create a climate for student growth in areas that are hard for teachers to impact through many traditional teaching models.

Benefits of Active Learning

1. **Active Learning involves everyone in the group.**
2. **Active Learning is student oriented, not teacher oriented.**
3. **Active Learning is process, not outcome oriented.**
4. **Active Learning is reinforced and directed through a discussion time.**
5. **Active Learning allows teachers to observe their students as they interact with each other.**
6. **Active Learning puts the burden of learning where it belongs - on the students themselves.**
7. **Active Learning allows students to have fun while they learn.**

Chapter Four

Overcoming Objections to Active Learning

"If teaching were only telling, my children would be incredibly brilliant; I've told them everything they need to know."
Howard G. Hendricks

There are always a lot of reasons not to do something different. Just the mere thought of trying something new is enough to cause some people to become nervous. Fortunately, Active Learning is not a radically new idea nor is it revolutionary in the education field. The reason I say fortunately, is because really new ideas regarding education take years and sometimes decades to become accepted. Since Active Learning has its base in Cooperative Learning, Experiential Learning and a number of other learning models, it can not really be called new. Many teachers have been using the ideas expressed in this book for some time. However, there are still a large number of teachers who choose not to experiment with anything that is different. Hopefully, their attitudes can still be changed.

Active Learning is simply another tool in the teacher's arsenal to attack the apathy that most students show for school. Notice I don't say learning. You can take a student who seems down right hostile towards education, put him in a situation where he wants to learn something of interest to him and he will work with great enthusiasm until he has mastered that area of interest. One example would be the football player who can't remember to do his homework but can memorize his blocking assignments for up to a hundred different plays. In the book *Cooperative Learning* by Spencer Kagan, he states that "learning is best promoted by being motivated to learn and being in a situation which allows learning to occur." Active Learning helps in both of these areas. The motivation for learning comes from the fact that the method of instruction has a fun side to it. Students want to participate in the lesson activity. The activity is also the vehicle by which the student is in a situation which allows learning to take place. It replaces passive learning with learning through involvement.

Active Learning is also a great vehicle to encourage interaction between your students. It is difficult not to be involved in the activity and with your fellow students when the success of your group depends on what you do and what happens between the members of the group. It is through this very interaction that learning takes place. It is learning that goes beyond the curriculum and into areas that affect the very being of your students and their success in life. In the book *Cooperation In The Classroom* by David Johnson, he relates that "extensive research comparing student interaction patterns clearly suggests that cooperation among students produces higher achievement, greater motivation to learn, more positive relationships among students, greater acceptance of differences, high self-esteem, and a number of other outcomes." Surely these are some of the outcomes that you would like to see in your students.

Another factor that research has shown is the fact that youth problems such as drugs, alcohol, teen sexual activity, suicide, etc., can not be dealt with in isolation. Prevention efforts in these areas must focus on people and the underlying factors that influence these types of behaviors. Active Learning deals with many of the underlying factors that have been shown to contribute to these areas of concern. These factors include communication skills, problem solving, formation of values, working together, goal setting and others. Many of the above listed acting out behaviors are a result of kids trying to clarify their uniqueness and discover what works for them. Patricia and Timothy Gerne, in their book *Substance Abuse Prevention Activities of Elementary Students*, state that "by the fourth grade other sources of information from peers, television and older siblings begin to challenge parents as the sole authority. Children, therefore, will need to learn necessary skills to clarify their own value judgements." It is through lesson plans that utilize such techniques as Active Learning that your students will be able to analyze exactly what they believe. We know that "scare tactics" do not make significant long-term behavioral changes in our youth. Only through the teaching and practicing of new and appropriate skills will we be able to successfully impact our youth. Active Learning gives you an avenue to present new skills and information in a manner that motivates students to become involved in their own learning process. Many of the lesson plans in this book

have a method for students to practice new skills and
then to evaluate what took place. It is during this discussion time that much of the applied learning takes
place.

"Researchers tell us that learning is more effective
when increasing numbers of the five basic senses are
involved", so states Edward Scannell in his book *Games
Trainers Play*. The more senses that are involved, the
better our retention of the information will be. This is
based on connectors. When we are able to connect information with something tangible, it is easier to recall
and apply. The more connectors we have, the easier it is
to transfer the information to different areas of our
lives. If we really understand something, then we can
apply it to situations that are similar but not necessar-
ily identical. This is the underlying goal of many of the
skills that we teach our youth. It is through Active
Learning that we can create many of these connectors.
In his book *Do It! Active Learning In Youth Ministry*,
Thom Schultz relates "Contrived experiences provide
almost as much learning potential as direct, purposeful
personal experience. These contrived activities can be
performed in the classroom. Games, simulations, and
role plays, when carefully planned and later debriefed,
can result in real learning with lasting implications."

Seven excuses for not using Active Learning

1. **Games are for kids.** Some teachers feel that their
   students are too old for activities that look a lot like
   playing games. They claim that their students are
   too sophisticated to be participating in such activities. In reality what you will find in many cases is

that the teacher doesn't like to play games; it has nothing to do with his students. Active Learning has been successful in classrooms across the country. Rich kids, poor kids, urban kids, suburban kids, old kids and young kids alike have found that, when properly presented, games can be fun.

2. **I need to tell my students what is important.** This is the philosophy behind lecturing. The students need to have information poured into their brain from a source that is more knowledgeable. I agree that for some kinds of information this is appropriate, but it is taken too far by too many. According to the publication *Communication Briefing*, "forty percent will forget what you've said after twenty minutes. Sixty percent of the kids will forget after half a day and a full ninety percent will forget after a week." Active Learning allows the students to tell each other what they thought was important with the teacher guiding those findings.

3. **Not enough content.** It is true that during the Active Learning lesson there will be less information taught than during some other types of teaching methods. This is why you need to have a balanced approach to teaching and use a variety of methods. When you discuss content, remember that there is a difference between what is taught and what is learned. Just because the information has been presented, doesn't mean that it has been internalized. Ice cream is great, but too much of it and the appeal is lost. Too much information or content presented at one time has the same effect. Our brain can only absorb so much at one time and then it begins to selectively remember what is being said or in some cases just turns off altogether.

4. **Too noisy.** Have you ever walked by a classroom and heard a lot of noise and even laughter coming out of the door, so you stuck your head in and there was the entire class up out of their seats? I know some people that would automatically assume that not only is learning not taking place, but that the teacher has lost control. We need to break out of the mold that quiet classrooms mean learning is taking place: Tell me how much noise day-dreaming makes. A room of thirty kids, all actively involved, produces noise. It also produces learning - more learning than a room of thirty kids sitting passively while the teacher drones on for extended periods of time.

5. **Takes too much time.** It depends on how you measure time. If you mean that an Active Learning lesson takes more time to complete than some other forms of teaching to get information to students, you are right. This teaching technique is not for large units of information that has to be given out quickly. It should be used when you want to affect a person's behavior, attitude, social skills or other life skills. The beauty of the technique is that once the teacher establishes the activity, the students teach themselves with guidance from the teacher. It may take longer than lecturing, but the outcome in terms of behavior change and retention are well worth it. The amount of time used is greater when your class is first experiencing Active Learning. Once the structure, format and process have been established, your class can move into the activity and the discussion in shorter and shorter time frames.

6. **Loss of control.** Teachers like to be in control of their students. Active Learning does not take away this control, but it does share that control with the students. This sharing takes place when the activity is underway. The teacher is there to monitor and be sure that the safety rules are followed, but basically stays in the background. However, even during the discussion time when control looks to be with the students, the teacher can maintain control since he is the one asking and directing the questions. A positive aspect of giving away some control is you get to see what your students are thinking instead of what the teacher is thinking.

7. **Too set in your old ways.** It doesn't matter how long you have been teaching, you will have heard the phrase "It's always been done that way." We are comfortable with the familiar and therefore, look with disfavor on anything that might change what we are used to. New ideas need to be approached one small step at a time. Since the Active Learning technique is not an entire new way of teaching or even a new curriculum, teachers can just get their feet wet and try out the water. Then as time goes by, and you feel more comfortable with the lesson plans, you can broaden your thinking and start adapting the lessons to better fit with your personality and the group of students you are teaching.

Chapter Five

Conducting an Active Learning Lesson

"In active learning, kids may learn lessons the teacher never envisioned. Because the leader trusts students to help create the learning experience, kids may venture into unforeseen discoveries. And often the teacher learns as much as the students."

Thom Schultz

Your enthusiasm for the activity will be the catalyst for the excitement of your students. If you approach the activity with an air of expectancy, this feeling will rub off on your students. Unfortunately the converse is also true: If you approach an activity with low key expectancy - so will your students. Active Learning, while being educational, is fun. Don't take the fun out of the experience by your attitude. Instead, let your attitude be part of the fun!

Tips on leading an activity

1. **Create a physically safe environment in which the activity can take place.** This can be dealt with by simply looking around the space you have

chosen to conduct the activity and checking for hazards. The hazards may be removed or pointed out so they can be avoided. If necessary, use spotters during the activity to be sure students don't run into objects or fall. Talk to the students about safety and remind them that activities can be dangerous if your directions are not followed correctly.

2. **Create a psychologically safe environment in which the activity can take place.** Psychological safety needs to be dealt with through the structure that you set up. There needs to be strict rules concerning put-downs, sarcasm, name calling, and other psyche-harming behaviors. Your tolerance towards allowing this kind of behavior will go a long way in setting the tone for the student's behavior during the activity.

3. **Establish a "freeze" command.** Work out some kind of signal word or noise, such as a whistle, that always means everyone needs to stop immediately. This signal can be used when a situation has become unsafe or if you wish to give further instructions. If you are close to a light switch, turning the lights off and on works really well. Just make sure that the students are not involved in anything physical, where a moment of darkness might cause a stumble or a fall.

4. **Remove students who refuse to cooperate.** If a student chooses to misbehave in such a manner as to make the activity unsafe, either physically or psychologically, they must be removed from the activity. You might want to set-up a warning system, such as one verbal warning before removing them, but do not let the actions of a couple of people ruin

the activity for the group as a whole. If the incident warrants such action, then immediate removal is certainly permissible. Allow them to rejoin the activity at the next logical break. Continue to monitor their behavior and discuss problems with them after the activity is over. Participation is a privilege, not a right and you should treat it as such. Be consistent in dealing with those that misbehave. The activities that are listed in the book are fun to do and most students will reconsider when they find themselves excluded.

5. **Directions should be short and to the point.** The longer you talk, the less they will listen. Remember that the central part of the lesson plan is the activity. You need to get them into the activity as quickly as possible. I find it best to give them directions after you have already formed them into whatever groups are needed for the particular activity. This breaks your directions into at least two sections. The first portion is how to form the groups needed, and the second is how to conduct the activity itself.

6. **If possible, demonstrate what you want them to do.** Modeling is always an excellent teaching tool. It helps them not only hear what they are to do, but see what they are to do. You don't have to show them step-by-step. This might defeat the purpose of the activity. You should only demonstrate difficult directions or those directions that would benefit most from a visual explanation.

7. **Be prepared for an imperfect first experience.** If this is the first time your students have even been involved in Active Learning or something similar,

they may not know how to respond. You will need to give much more guidance to your group the first few times they experience this type of learning. Many of them are used to being told exactly what to do and staying in their seats to do it. The less structured atmosphere of Active Learning may be difficult for them the first few times it is tried. Don't despair! This is normal and will pass. Keep trying; the rewards in increased student participation and retention of content are well worth the seeming chaos in the beginning activities.

The teacher's role in Active Learning

1. **Be personally enthusiastic.** No one else is going to be excited about the activity if you come across as bored with the whole thing.

2. **Maintain control over your students during the activity.** Keep a close watch on the students as they participate in the activity. This is not a time to correct papers, fix the bulletin board or any other housekeeping chores. Your full attention needs to be with the kids. It only takes a moment for an unsafe procedure to take place or a breakdown to occur in the safe environment.

3. **Be the time keeper.** Some activities will require time periods to be kept. The teacher should be the one that does this rather than assigning it to a student. Sometimes you need to adjust the time to better fit the ability of the group. Many times this does not become apparent until the activity is underway. If you are the time keeper, you can make appropriate adjustments to better accommodate your stu-

dents. Use your inner sense to know when to make the time shorter or longer to allow the activity to have more impact.

4. **Be flexible.** Too many times we think we know just how an activity should proceed, and when something different happens we panic. Active Learning has many different paths it can follow. As long as there is learning taking place, let the activity continue. Watch for unexpected teachable moments; they may come at any time during the activity.

5. **Watch, Watch, Watch!** Since each group has their own distinct personality, they will add something different to every activity. You need to be aware of the dynamics that are taking place: Who is doing what and how are their actions impacting the rest of the group? Your observations will form the thrust of the discussion that follows the activity. You may even want to write down some notes to help you remember significant actions or dialogue that took place during the activity which you can use during the discussion time to help the class process what took place.

Chapter Six

Discussion: The How and The Why

"Conversation is the laboratory and workshop of the student."

Ralph Waldo Emerson

There are many terms used to define what takes place after an activity. These terms include discussions, processing and debriefing. All mean essentially the same thing, which is to talk about what just happened and to determine its application to real life. Carmine Consalvo in her book *Workplay*, describes it this way, "Processing or debriefing refers to the questioning and discussion that follows the game. It strives to elicit critical reflection based on observations regarding what happened in terms of both external interactions and internal reactions."

The role of the teacher during the discussion is a critical one. The teacher needs to assume the role of guide and participant rather than traffic cop, unless something is said that will damage the discussion or is so blatantly incorrect that it needs clarification. If clarification is needed, see if asking the students for clarification is possible, rather than jumping in and stopping the flow of the discussion. More clarification and teacher involvement will be needed with younger students and even with older students when you are getting your class used to the discussion format. Skill must be used to steer the discussion rather than control it or dominate it. A good healthy discussion flows around the teacher not back and forth from teacher to student.

The teacher has basically two roles during the discussion. The first role is to set-up the format by deciding how people will take turns talking and provide a safe environment for opinions. Your second role is one of asking questions. This will consist of opening with a question that reviews the activity which just took place and then to continue asking questions that help the students explore the activity and apply it to their lives. If you wish a free exchange of ideas during the discussion time you must be sure that you do not interject your own opinion either overtly or covertly. If this occurs, the students will start searching for the "right answers" based on what they think the teacher wants rather than looking for what each other thinks. Be careful of what you say after a student has had a turn. If you enthusiastically nod your head, say "great answer", or any other comment that can be interpreted as complimentary then you affirm that answer. Instead, adopt a standard set of remarks that show you heard the student, appreciate their comments and that they have finished making their remarks. A simple "thank you" or " O.K." will accomplish this.

Do not be afraid of silence during a discussion. Too many times teachers ask a question and then, when their students are thinking, jump in with another question. Give them some time to collect their thoughts and formulate an answer. If you truly believe that you have asked a question that is too difficult to answer, then wait a short while and rephrase the same question so they won't have to start thinking all over again. Once the discussion has concluded, you should resume the role of the teacher and summarize what has been said and restate the important concepts that have been brought out.

A discussion emphasizes learning instead of teaching. Students are not only thinking about the issues, but they are also learning to ask the right questions of themselves and others. This is the beginning of critical thinking which is the basis for many of the skills needed to deal with the issues that will trouble them as they work towards adulthood and independence. Research has shown that information which is discussed, rather than just heard via a lecture, is remembered longer and becomes more meaningful to students. This is due to the fact that students are required to rephrase the information in their own language. When students share aloud, they become more confident in their opinions. This helps shape their thinking and eventually their behavior. It is better that their opinions are shared and shaped in the classroom where you have some control over the situation, rather than the streets where a voice of reason may not be present. Your presence has some impact on what is said and the direction of the discussion can be tempered by the questions you ask.

A discussion can reinforce concepts your students already have but were afraid to admit because they felt no one else felt the same way. This is a good exercise in positive peer pressure. A teacher can preach the evils of anti-social behavior and not reach kids, but if a classmate says the same thing the impact is greatly increased. A discussion can also help nurture communication skills. We know that good communication is the foundation for success in life. A good discussion can educate your students by its process as well as by what is said. The chance to share ideas and opinions creates the opportunity for kids to become better communicators - as speakers, listeners and thinkers.

Benefits of having discussions

1. **Students learn to take turns speaking.**

2. **Students learn to value each person's opinion and experiences.**

3. **Students can experiment with new thoughts opinions and ideas in a safe environment.**

4. **Students can develop the skills of observation, analysis and logic.**

5. **Students learn to clarify and review what they have learned.**

6. **Students will learn opinions that differ from their own and can expand their body of information to create new opinions.**

7. **The teacher can evaluate a student's knowl-**

edge about and understanding of the information being discussed.

8. The teacher is able to hear what his/her students are thinking, feeling and experiencing in a non-threatening environment.

9. The teacher can have dialogue with a large number of people at one time.

10. Allows for structured exploration of a topic using comments that the participants think are important rather than just what the teacher feels is significant.

11. Is student oriented, yet teacher controlled.

12. Very flexible and adaptable to varying age groups, maturity levels and topics.

The basics of starting a discussion

Ground rules for a great discussion

1. Personal or sensitive information stays in the room and is not to be repeated to friends, family or others.

2. There will be absolutely no put downs, sarcasm or humor directed towards or at the expense of another person.

3. There is no such thing as a dumb question, comment or opinion. Everyone has the right

to ask or say what they want as long as it is
appropriately expressed.

4. Individuals can be encouraged to talk, but no
    one is forced to talk.

5. Out of respect for the speaker, only one person
    talks at a time.

6. Be sure that you have prepared your basic
    questions ahead of time.

7. Try to get as many people talking during the
    first few minutes of the discussion as possible.

8. Do not be afraid to let the discussion go off
    track as long as it is filling needs. The stu-
    dents may have a better idea of what is rele-
    vant to them than you do. Use another ques-
    tion to refocus the discussion rather than
    pointing out the fact that the discussion is off
    track.

9. If the class is in excessive agreement, play the
    devil's advocate to stimulate critical thinking.

10. Don't be afraid of silence.

The magic of questions

I can not stress too strongly the importance of the
discussion time following an activity. The activity is not
complete without it. If you see that time is running out,
cut down on the activity rather than eliminate or dilute

the discussion. Questions are the focal point of a discussion. What you ask and how you ask it will greatly determine the success of the discussion and the concepts explored.

The first rule of any discussion is for you to determine what direction you want the discussion to go. This keeps significant issues from being lost when the discussion becomes side tracked. The question or comment a teachers uses to start the discussion is important because it sets the trend for the rest of the discussion. Good discussion questions will focus on a person's opinion, experience or feelings. There are no right or wrong answers for these types of questions. Good discussion-starting questions will begin with words such as why, explain, how, what do you think, etc. This type of phrasing lets the students know that there is something to discuss rather than a specific answer being looked for.

Active Learning becomes a learning experience when we reflect upon what we have done, what impact that has and how to apply it to our lives. This can be summed up in three questions - What happened? So what? and What next?. To expand these questions just a bit, think of the three areas that they cover. The first set of questions reflect on the activity itself. What just happened here and how do you feel about it? The second area concerns what we can learn from the activity. The third is how we will be different because of what we have experienced. These areas can be explored with three types of questions. The first is "Launching Questions." These get the discussion going. Everyone participated in the activity so everyone can answer these questions. The second is "Understanding Questions." These will ask about feelings and concepts that were brought out during the activity. The last is "Applying Questions." These will ask how the facts, concepts, and principles from the activity can be applied to their lives.

Questions to avoid

1. **Questions that have a right or wrong answer.**

2. **Questions that can be answered yes or no.**

3. **Long wordy questions where the meaning is forgotten before you even stop asking.**

4. **A question within a question.**

5. **Questions that are either - or.**

6. **Questions that have an obvious answer.**

7. **Questions that are too general or too vague.**

8. **Questions that the students do not have enough experience to answer.**

Questions that can be used to keep your discussion going

Sometimes after you have thrown out your thought provoking opening question, the discussion starts to run into some rough spots. This is where your question asking skills will become important. You can use questions to help clarify statements, to look at an issue more deeply, to redirect the discussion to another student or to draw someone into the discussion.

"Can you give us an example..."
"What did you mean when you said..."
"What makes you believe that?"
"Please explain what you just said."
"What reason do you have to feel that way?"
"What part of the activity do you base your opinion on?
"Could you expand on that?"
"What other feelings did you feel?"
"Please tell us more about..."
"What did you mean by...?"
"What else can you add?"
"Susan, what do you think about John's answer?"
"Jesse, tell us what you think."
"Well, we have heard from Mindy. Greg what do you think?"
"Thanks Armando. Jessica what do you think?"
"Brandon you have said a great deal. What do others think?"

Getting kids to talk

Some students will hesitate to speak in a group because they are shy or they feel that their contribution is not very valuable. They feel that the comments and opinions of others are more important than theirs. You can use a variety of techniques to draw them into the discussion that is taking place or future discussions. Realize that everyone benefits from a discussion, not just those that talk. Your students will learn just by listening to the questions and hearing the discussion that takes place.

1. **Start with questions that are non-threatening and not too personal.**

2. Use questions that ask for opinions rather than facts.

3. Use an activity as a basis for the discussion so everyone has the same experience to draw from.

4. Have the students write down their opinions and then read them to the class for comment.

5. Ask for a comment from someone who has not contributed yet.

6. Ask a student what they thought of another student's comment.

7. After class talk to students who are habitually quiet. Ask them some questions and when they answer, explain that those are worthwhile opinions and you would like to have them expressed so everyone can benefit from them.

Chapter Seven

Discussion Formats

"Processing or debriefing refers to the questioning and discussion that follows the game. It strives to elicit critical reflection based on observations regarding what happened in terms of both external interactions and internal reactions."
Carmine M. Consalvo

Many factors play a role in having a good discussion; Such simple things as the set-up of the room can impact the success of your discussion. If you want to generate discussion among your students, the best seating arrangement is one that allows all of the students to see each other. It does not take very long for your students to rearrange themselves into a circle or a square. After practicing a couple of times, most classes can reduce the time and noise associated with this change to a minimum.

Where the teacher stands is another factor. If the group is in rows facing the teacher, then the teacher is the focal point of all of the comments. If the students are seated in a circle and the teacher stands at one end, the teacher will still dominate the discussion. If you want the discussion to be as student oriented as possible, then the teacher should sit in the circle with the students. Many teachers start their class off with the teacher being the dominant person in the discussion. Then as the class becomes more comfortable with the discussion format, the teacher moves off of center stage and allows the discussion to become more student centered. The timing of such a move will depend upon the age, maturity and ability level of your students.

There are many different formats that can be used for discussions other than the traditional "teacher ask - student answer" format. A few of these are listed in this chapter. Once again, I urge you to use your own creativity to adapt these formats or create one of your own for use in your classroom. I would recommend that you vary the format of your discussions, as students enjoy change in their learning environment.

Large Group: This is basically the traditional format where the teacher asks the questions and the students respond. This is the easiest format to use in the beginning because the students are already familiar with it. This format also allows you the most control over the discussion and the class.

Small Groups: Divide your class into groups of about five to seven students. Have them spread out around the room and discuss the activity. You can give them one question and have them discuss it until you call time and then give them a second question, or you can put all of the questions on the board or on a hand out for them to answer in their groups. If you want the class to stay together and work on the same question at the same time, you could put the questions on an overhead transparency and reveal each question as you feel the class is ready to move on. For accountability, you can randomly ask one or two groups to share with the rest of the class the main issues discussed in their groups.

Buzz Groups: Divide your class into groups of between five to seven students. Have each group select a leader and a recorder. The leader is responsible for keeping the discussion going and the recorder writes down the group's ideas. You can use the same steps as found in the "Small Group" format for asking the questions and keeping the groups together. When you have covered all of your questions, have the recorder or a designated spokesperson from each group share their comments. After that, you may want to open up each question for large group discussion or follow-up with additional questions for the large group or the buzz groups.

Partners: The more students that you can involve in the discussion time the more one and all will learn. Have your students pair up with a partner. Once again you can give them a list of questions, have questions on the board and reveal them one at a time, or ask questions one at a time for them to discuss between themselves. Randomly ask pairs to share what they discussed. You could then follow-up with additional questions for the entire group or for them to discuss further with their partner.

Written Answers: Some students do not react well to the pressure of a discussion. They need private time to collect their thoughts and form their answers. Have your class answer the basic questions that you would like to ask in writing before you open up the discussion. Let them keep the paper in front of them and read the answers they wrote when called upon. For some reason, students seem to feel more comfortable reading an answer. This works especially well with groups who are just learning how to discuss.

Written Comments: Again, have your students write down their answers to your questions. Then collect the papers and read some of the answers to your first question. Ask students to comment on what you have read. Then go onto the second question and repeat the process. This allows you to hear from students who would not normally respond during the discussion time. It also disassociates the comment from the person. Comments can be read and discussed while the contributor remains anonymous. This is a good method to try if your class is reluctant to share their opinions in a group setting.

Agree - Disagree Continuum: This format requires your students to physically commit themselves to a point of view. In your room, assign one wall of the class as the "Strongly Agree" side and the other wall as the "Strongly Disagree" side. Read a statement and tell your students to line up between the walls according to how much they agree or disagree with the statement that you just read. They can arrange themselves from one side of the room to the other, with those in the middle having opinions that both agree and disagree with the statement you read. Once they have arranged themselves, ask various students to explain why they chose to stand where they did. Start with one side of the room, then go to the other and finish with those in the middle. Ask at the end if anyone would like to reconsider where they chose to stand and ask them to explain why. Then read a second statement and have them once again choose where to stand.

This is an excellent way to have the entire class participate, even if they all don't get a chance to explain why they chose their particular spot to stand. Simply by having to move from one spot to another, they had to think about the question. It is also a good activity to talk about peer pressure and what impact where friends chose to stand had on students. The most difficult part of this format for the teacher is writing a good statement. It must be controversial enough so some students will agree and others will disagree. Remember that you do not use questions, but rather statements.

Thumbs Up: A less time consuming variation to the above format works with a signal to designate how much you agree or disagree with a statement. One good signal makes use of the thumb. You read the statement and then the class agrees by giving the "thumbs-up" sign, disagrees by giving the "thumbs-down" sign and is in the middle by pointing the thumb sideways. You may call on them to explain their particular choice. This format does not have the same impact as lining up because students can hide their signals or not commit.

Videotape: As an aid for getting a discussion going, videotape the activity the students were involved in. Show the video tape to the class and stop it at strategic points. Ask the class what they saw going on and discuss various segments.

Tokens: This format helps when you have a few students who dominate the discussions. Give everyone a certain number of tokens or chips. Each time they have a turn during the discussion, they must surrender one of their tokens. When they are out of tokens, they can not say anything else. You may give out more tokens as often you like.

Flying Ball: If your class is having trouble with the concept of only one person speaking at a time, this is a fun format. Get a small nerf ball or similar object that has enough weight to it to be thrown, but not enough weight to hurt people. The only person that may talk is the one that has the object. It is thrown from speaker to speaker and physically shows who has the floor at the time. This is especially good with younger classes.

Chapter Eight

Using the Active Learning Lesson Plans

"You can lead a horse to water, but you can't make him drink. Wrong! You can feed him salt."
Howard G. Hendricks

These lesson plans were written for individuals, such as teachers and others who work with young people, who might not have a lot of experience in leading an Active Learning lesson. Those who are experienced in this or similar teaching techniques, will find the following explanations very basic. Those who find this teaching technique as a new or unfamiliar challenge will discover more use for these instructions. I would encourage all teachers to use these lesson plans as only a starting point for your own creativity.

Topic Area: A listing of the topics for which discussion questions have been developed. If more than one topic is listed, there is a comma between the topics. You should rarely try to address more than one topic, unless it is alcohol and other drugs, during a single lesson. Use your own judgement about how many topics your students can handle during one activity and discussion time. There are many more topics that can be addressed for each of these lesson plans than I have indicated. In many cases, topic application is limited only by your own imagination and ingenuity.

Concept: An explanation of why this activity is important and how it can be applied to your students. This section will give you a basis for information that should be presented before the activity. Remember that activities should not stand alone. Introductory material needs to be given to help in understanding and applying the concept that is experienced during the activity. Without a strong introduction and solid follow-up, an activity becomes just fun rather than a learning opportunity. However, don't go too far when introducing the activity. You want this to be a discovery process; let the students experience and then discuss the activity. Major concepts will be more significant if they are discovered during and after the activity by the students rather than by having you explain the important concepts or key points to them.

Method: Only two classifications are used. One is Classroom Demonstration. Here the teacher undertakes an activity in front of the class. One or more students may be involved in the demonstration. The second method is Classroom Activity. Under this format the entire class will be directly involved in the activity. The teacher's role will be to facilitate the activity and be sure a safe environment, both physically and psychologically, is provided. Consideration should be taken as to how much room will be needed for a particular activity. You may have to rearrange chairs and tables in your room or even move to a larger facility, which could be indoors or outdoors.

Time Frame: This is only an estimate based on the past history of these activities. Your class may take longer or shorter. Some consideration might need to be given to how quickly your group understands directions and can set-up for the activity. Extra time can be consumed when teams are chosen, room arrangements made or materials distributed. Once your group gets accustomed to the Active Learning format, they will become more adept at the logistics of getting ready. Remember you need to allow time for introductory material and follow-up discussion time. This time has not been figured into the time frame estimate.

Materials Needed: Each activity has been designed with as few materials needed as possible. If handouts are called for, they will be found at the end of the activity. You can photocopy as many classroom sets for your own use as you need. Most materials are easily found and cost very little. Extras should be on hand in case they are needed during the activity. I would hate to see an activity fall apart just because a prop is misplaced or broken.

Activity: This is a description of how to conduct the activity. Instructions are given on how to set up the format of the activity. I decided to use the gender neutral "he" in writing the instructions. Originally I tried to use the he/she sentence construction. However, some activities became very confusing with this format so I went back to the old style of the generic "he". This may not be as politically correct, but I can guarantee you that it is to the benefit of the reader.

I would suggest that you go through the steps of each activity before you try to conduct it with your group. Sometimes things that sound easy when you read them, suddenly become confusing when you try to put them into practice. If you get in the middle of an activity and find something not working correctly, stop and give further instructions to make changes which will work. Be sure that you can explain the activity clearly and easily. It is best if you can demonstrate movements that might be difficult before you ask your students to try them. If teams are called for, the numbers I have given are flexible. Decide what would work best for your group. If you have an odd number that will not make even teams, you can have one or more people go more than once to even things out. If it is a partners activity then you will have to participate.

Don't try to do too many activities in one day. For these to be most effective, each one should be given full attention. If you do too many, one right after the other, the students start to look at them as games rather than learning activities. The discussion time is the key. If you take the proper time to discuss each activity, then the opportunity for life changing learning will present itself.

Variations: Not many of these have been included. Your willingness to think and be creative is the only thing holding you back from making dozens of variations from these listed activities. I encourage you to send any variations or new activity ideas to me to be included in future publications and workshops. Some of the ideas in this book were given to me by innovative teachers. Let me help you share your creativity with others.

Discussion Ideas: Just a few questions to help you get started. These questions will help you follow-up with the topics listed at the start of the lesson plan. The discussion time is absolutely necessary to complete the activity. Spend some time before you conduct the activity to think about the questions you would like to ask and in what order you would like to ask them. Watch your students during the activity and you will have questions pop into your mind. Try to keep most of your questions open ended with no right or wrong answers. The questions that I have listed are not in any particular order nor are they meant to be used first to last. Use these questions as a jumping off point and then use others to explore important issues that came up during the activity or during the discussion.

Appropriate Age Levels: You will notice that this category has been left off of the lesson plans. The reason for this omission is simple. I could give suggested grade levels, but then you might not read a lesson that could easily be adapted to your grade by simply changing one aspect of the activity. Another reason for not suggesting grade levels is some classes are very advanced and some are not. By not predetermining what grade level each lesson plan fits, you can make your own decision based on what you know about your class rather than what I think about a lesson. So go ahead and read them all. Use what works and change what doesn't. Have fun!

***Check the back of the book for information outlining a half-day and full-day workshop, where you can have hands-on experience in conducting Active Learning lesson plans.

Chapter Nine

Active Learning Lesson Plans

"Learning can take place at three levels— cognitive, affective or psychomoter. The acquisition of knowledge, attitudes, or skills can be expedited through the selective utilization of an appropriate game."

Edward E. Scannell

"Yes you can learn about a football game by watching it on television. But you'll learn more and remember the game longer if you join the team and play."

Thom Schultz

A MILLION DOLLARS

TOPIC AREAS: Drugs, Values

CONCEPT: Weekly, if not daily, we read reports in the newspaper of drug busts that net millions of dollars worth of illegal drugs. When we hear about a million dollars or more of drugs being confiscated, does that really make the impact on our thinking that it should? A million dollars is a lot more money than most of us will ever have at one time, so how can we really comprehend what it represents? To understand the drug problem in America, the issue of money must be discussed. This activity will help your students realize the magnitude of the drug problem as it relates to money and lost production hours from our work force. Why would people sell a product that destroys the lives of so many individuals? Why would people risk long jail terms to smuggle drugs into the country or set-up elaborate processing or growing laboratories? We need to make the term "a million dollars" mean something concrete to our youth.

METHOD: Classroom Activity

TIME FRAME: 30 minutes plus discussion time

MATERIALS NEEDED:
- Catalogs from mail order houses (places such as Sears will donate catalogs to your classroom if you explain their use)
- Brochures from car dealers and luxury item outlets

- Classified sections of the newspaper (Multiple copies can be obtained from your local newspaper, especially day old editions)
- At least one calculator for each team of three people

ACTIVITY: Divide your group into teams of three. Explain that each group has one million dollars to spend. They may buy anything that can be found in any of the catalogs, newspapers or brochures that you have provided for them. If you live in a high priced housing market, you may have to eliminate a house from the list of what they can purchase. Catalogs, newspapers and brochures may be traded between groups. They may only purchase one of any item. This means that they may buy three automobiles, but each one must be a different kind. They may buy three television sets, but each one must be a different kind. Two out of the three people in each group must agree before the item can be purchased. They will need to keep a written list of the items purchased and the amount paid for each. They will need to keep a running total of money spent so they will know when they reach a million dollars. The groups will find that spending a million dollars is not easy.

DISCUSSION IDEAS:
- What happened during this activity?
- What problems did you encounter?
- How did you decide in your group on what items to purchase?
- Did you find a million dollars easy or hard to spend? Explain
- What kinds of items did you purchase?
- When people become rich, are they satisfied or do they always want more money? Explain

- What does this activity tell us about the drug business?
- Explain how this activity makes the drug business look appealing.
- Why would people risk jail time for selling illegal drugs?
- Why would people risk jail time for manufacturing or growing illegal drugs?
- How do you think money affects the decision of people who don't have very much, when they are asked to deliver drugs for a dealer?
- With profits in the drug business being so large, do you think we can ever stop the drug business? Why or why not?
- How could we make the drug business not so profitable? How would your answers affect the rest of society?
- Why does the average person who doesn't use illegal drugs even have to be concerned with the drug business?
- What effect does the illegal drug business have on day-to-day life for the average person?

ALL THUMBS

TOPIC AREAS: Alcohol, Other Drugs

CONCEPT: When someone is under the influence of alcohol or other drugs, they will not be able to perform at the same standard as when they were not under the influence. Our country loses millions of dollars each year in the workplace due to lowered productivity caused by the use of alcohol and other drugs. Manual dexterity, decision making and problem solving skills are diminished when the body is under the influence. Lowered productivity or the inability to produce means someone else at work must pick up or cover for the impaired worker. Research has shown that even when a person is not legally drunk or is only feeling the after effects of a drug, his performance can be diminished. This diminished capacity is not only detrimental in the workplace, but also on the highways where slowed thinking or reactions can cause injury and death.

METHOD: Classroom Activity

TIME FRAME: 20 minutes plus discussion time

MATERIALS NEEDED:
- One pair of gloves for each team of five
- One 1 1/2 inch in length round head 10/32 diameter machine screw (or similar) for each team of five
- One nut that will fit onto the screw for each team of five
- A stopwatch or watch with a second hand on it

ACTIVITY: Divide your group into teams of five. Have them sit in a circle. Give each group a threaded machine screw and a nut. Explain that each person must thread the nut onto the machine screw all the way to the end and then thread it back off of the machine screw. When they have finished, the machine screw and nut are passed to the next person on the team and they are to repeat the action. The machine screw and nut must pass all the way around the circle being threaded on and off by each team member. Use a watch to time each team and see how long it takes for them to complete the task. For round number two, pass out a pair of gloves to each team. They are to repeat the activity while wearing the gloves. The one pair of gloves is passed from team member to team member to wear during their turn to thread the nut on the machine screw. Once again, time the activity and compare each team's score with the time they had in the previous round. Repeat the activity a third time with only the first, third and fifth person on each team having to wear gloves. Once again time the activity and compare results.

DISCUSSION IDEAS:
- What did you see happening in this activity?
- How hard was it to thread the nut when you were not wearing gloves?
- How hard was it to thread the nut when you were wearing gloves?
- As a team member, how did you feel about the performance of those wearing gloves when you were not?
- As a team member, how did you feel about your performance when you were wearing gloves and others on the team did not have to?

- How would you feel about working with a person who could not properly perform their job because they were under the influence?
- What should employers do with employees that come to work impaired?
- How can we relate this activity to alcohol and other drug use?
- List some of the jobs where performance would be impacted by alcohol and other drug use.

ALL TIED UP

TOPIC AREAS: Addiction, Habits

CONCEPT: No one wakes up in the morning and decides to become a drug addict that day. Habits and addiction are usually slow processes that build up over time. They sneak up without us even realizing what we are getting into. The first time we do something we may not even think much about it, but as that activity is repeated over and over again our body and mind becomes used to it. The problems associated with habits and addictions are usually not ones that occur overnight, but rather one small step at a time.

METHOD: Classroom Demonstration

TIME FRAME: 7 minutes plus discussion time

MATERIALS NEEDED:
- A pair of gloves
- A roll of extra lightweight string or sewing thread

ACTIVITY: Have one student come up to the front of the room. Have him put on the gloves. These will protect his hands against small cuts and make the demonstration look even more impressive. Then have him put his hands out in front of him about stomach level, ten inches apart. The palms should be facing each other. Explain to the class that you want to show how habits and most addictions are formed. Take the string and wrap it one time around his hands and then tie it so that a circle around his hands is formed. Ask him to try and break the string. He should be able to do this very easily. If he can't then you bought string that was way too strong. Explain to the class that this is just like the first time you do something. It is not hard for you to stop that activity. Now wrap the string around his hands two times. Have him try to break the strings. He should still be able to break them. Explain to the class that it may be harder, but he could still stop the activity if he wanted to. Keep wrapping the string around his hands and having him break it until he no longer can do so. This is showing that habits and most addictions do not occur all at once. They sneak up on you one repeated behavior at a time until you have no control over the behavior, but it has control over you.

DISCUSSION IDEAS:
* What happened when there was just one string around his hands?
* What happened when there were two strings around his hands?
* What happened as I added strings around his hands?
* What was the final result of adding the strings?
* What can this activity tell us about habits and addiction?
* What are some habits that we have?
* Are all habits bad for us?
* What are some of the things that we can become addicted to?
* Are all addictions bad for us?
* What is the difference between a habit and an addiction?

(Webster's: Habit - an acquired mode of behavior that has become nearly or completely involuntary.

Addiction - a compulsive physiological need or dependence on a substance or behavior.)

AUCTION BLOCK

TOPIC AREAS: Goal Setting, Values

CONCEPT: We work toward the goals that we think are important. Part of the goal setting process is determining what is important and why. It is in this formulation of goals that our values play an important role. We are willing to put time, effort and money into the areas that we feel are important to us. These areas can change over time as our values change. The pre-teen and teen years are certainly times of transition when different sets of values are experimented with. These changing values can be a significant factor in the goals that we keep and the ones we discard or reevaluate.

METHOD: Classroom Activity

TIME FRAME: 20 minutes plus discussion time

MATERIALS NEEDED:
- One auction list handout per person
- One pencil per person

ACTIVITY: Give each participant an auction list handout. Explain to them that they have $2,000 to bid on the items from the list. The items will be auctioned off one at a time. All bids must be in increments of $100. The item will go to the highest bidder. Run it just like a regular auction. Give the individuals time before the auction begins to look down their list and see which items they wish to bid on and how much they think they might offer. This amount should be written in the column marked "Proposed Bid". They are not held to that amount, but it gets them thinking about the items and their worth to them. During the auction have everyone keep track of how much the item was actually sold for and who the winning bidder was. After you have auctioned off all of the items, there will be some students with money left.

Tell the students before you begin that anyone who has $500 or more left at the end of the auction can spend their entire remaining amount on one of three secret boxes after the auction is complete. These three boxes can be sold to as many people as have the money and wish to buy them. This part is not a bidding process. Do not tell them what is contained in each of the three boxes. The three boxes contain the following: Box number one - You bought a lottery ticket and won a million dollars; Box number two - You dropped out of high school and took a job at below minimum wage with no chance of advancement; Box number three - You graduated from high school, went to college and took a job that pays a reasonable salary, but you dislike what you do.

This activity is played to show where our values and goals lie. What you were willing to spend your money on gives you an idea of what you think is important. Those with money left over at the end have no real strong goals as of yet, or at least none that were on the list. The secret boxes at the end of the auction are used to show that if you don't know where you are headed, then you will just end up with whatever life hands you. The reason you had money at the end of the auction could be because you didn't feel strong enough about anything on the list to bid all you had. Goal setting helps give direction to your life. As you mature and find your values or lifestyle changing, your goals can be adjusted accordingly.

DISCUSSION IDEAS:
*   What items sold for the highest amounts?
*   What items sold for the lowest amounts?
*   In what category would you put the higher selling items?
*   In what category would you put the lower selling items?
*   Why did some items sell for more than others?
*   Why were some people willing to bid a higher amount for some items than they were willing to bid on other items?
*   What does this tell us about the value people place on different things in life?
*   Why didn't everyone want the same items?
*   Were there any items you really wanted to bid on, but were afraid of what the other people in the group would think or say about you?
*   Were any items not bid upon? or had a very low bid? Why?
*   What does the overall bidding tell us about our group?
*   Does this type of activity give us any indication about what we feel is of value to us in life?
*   How did you feel when all of your money was gone?
*   How did you feel if you had money left at the end of the auction?
*   Did any of you consciously save money to be able to purchase a secret box? Why or why not?
*   How did those people who bid on the secret boxes feel about their purchase?
*   How can we apply this activity to real life?
*   What are some of the things that you would be willing to really work for to accomplish?

AUCTION LIST

Each person has a total of $2,000 to bid with.

Item to be auctioned	Proposed Bid	Actual Bid	Purchaser
1. To be a famous rock star			
2. To never be sick			
3. To be extremely smart			
4. To be a famous sports star			
5. To be beautiful			
6. To be President of the USA			
7. To have a great looking body			
8. To be a famous model			
9. To be a school teacher			
10. To graduate from a famous college			
11. To never have pimples			
12. To help underprivileged children			
13. To be a doctor			
14. To be a successful politician			
15. To raise happy children			

Item to be auctioned	Proposed Bid	Actual Bid	Purchaser
16. To be a successful artist			
17. To live a long life			
18. To own whatever car I would like			
19. To marry a good looking person			
20. To have a successful business			
21. To live in a mansion			
22. To be liked by everyone			
23. To be a famous movie star			
24. To help the homeless problem			
25. To have a lot of close friends			
26. To be happy in life			
27. To be a millionaire			
28. To help others			
29. To travel around the world			
30. To have a great relationship with my parents			

Use the bottom of the page to record how much money you have spent so far on successful bids. Remember to stop bidding when you have spent $2,000. If you have

$500 or more left at the end of the auction, you can purchase one of the secret boxes. Each secret box has an undisclosed future in it. Each of the three boxes may be purchased by as many people as have the money left to do so.

AWESOME LAP SIT

TOPIC AREA: Communication, Working Together

CONCEPT: As we talk with each other we need to remember that we must not only worry about what we are going to say, but also concentrate on what the other person is saying. If we just talk then we are not really communicating, we are just telling. This exercise shows the importance of concerning ourselves with what the other person is doing and finding out that by doing this, we are also taking care of ourselves.

METHOD: Classroom Activity

TIME FRAME: 15 minutes plus discussion time

MATERIALS NEEDED: None

ACTIVITY: Have your group stand in a circle. Have them all turn to the right and take small steps in towards the center until they are real close to the person in front of them and the person behind them. If the circle has become an egg shape then you need to move people around until you have a perfect circle. Have them put their hands on the waist of the person in front of them. Stress safety before you do this activity. Be sure that everyone is working together and takes responsibility for their own actions.

Now on the count of three have each person slowly sit down. Each person should concentrate on helping the person in front of them down onto their lap. Notice I did not say to worry about the lap you are going to be sitting on. This responsibility belongs to the person behind you. You worry about the person who is going to sit on your lap. If everyone sits down together and everyone helps guide each other onto their lap, an amazing thing happens. No one falls down and the circle is complete. If someone was not properly positioned right in front of someone else, then you may have had a collapse in one section. If the activity did not work, then restructure it and try again.

The key to this activity is that everyone must take care of each other. It doesn't matter how heavy the person is that sits on you or how little the person is that you sit on. As long as everyone works together the weight is evenly distributed and no one will be squished or fall over. If you really want to challenge your group there are a couple of more activities for them to try. After they have successfully sat down, have them raise their hands in the air and give themselves a round of applause. This proves that the circle is really sturdy. Going even further, have them try to walk around the circle. Get everyone to move their outside foot at the same time, then the inside foot and for the really brave continue in this fashion in a circular pattern.

DISCUSSION IDEAS:
- What were you thinking as I first explained the activity?
- Did you have any trouble concentrating on the person who was going to sit on your lap?
- Were you too worried about where you were going to sit?
- How did the activity go the first time we tried it?
- How did you feel when I asked you to raise your hands and clap?

- How did you feel when I asked you to try walking?
- What corrections did we have to make before it worked?
- What would have happened if everyone did not work together?
- How does this activity show working together?
- In what areas of our lives do we do better when we work together?
- What can this activity tell us about good communication?
- In what areas of our lives does good communication help us?
- Have you ever had a situation where one person was not helping the group?
- What happened in this situation? What was the outcome? Were feelings hurt?

BACK ART

TOPIC AREA: Communication

CONCEPT: Saying what you mean and hearing what is said are problems that we have in any communication between two people. You can imagine how these problems can escalate when you have more than two people involved. An example would be a comment or set of instructions that passes through a number of people and the interpretation that each person puts on the information. Rumors are certainly a good illustration of this problem; they seem to grow bigger and better with each telling.

METHOD: Classroom Activity

TIME FRAME: 15 to 20 minutes plus discussion time

MATERIALS NEEDED:
- A pencil, magic marker or crayon for each group of five to six people
- Five or six blank pieces of notebook sized paper for each group of five to six people

ACTIVITY: Divide your class into groups of five to six people. Have each group sit in a single file line facing the front of the room. This can be done sitting on the floor (my favorite), sitting in chairs or even standing. The last person in line from each team, meets with the teacher and is shown a picture to draw. All the teams are shown the same picture, at the same time. After seeing the picture, they go back to their team and place themselves at the end of the line.

At the starting command, they use their finger to draw the picture that they saw on the back of the student in front of them. Once they are done drawing, the person in front of them tries to draw the same thing on the back of the person in front of him. This continues until it reaches the first person in line. He draws what he thinks was drawn on his back onto a piece of paper. When he finishes drawing, he raises his hand and puts down his pencil and turns his paper over so no one else can see his drawing. The teacher notes the order that the teams finished.

After all of the teams have finished, each picture should be held up for the team and class to see how well they did. The teacher should hold up the original so the drawings can be compared. The picture of the team that finished first should be checked by the teacher or judge to see how closely it resembles the original picture. If it is close enough in the eyes of the judge, then that team gets a point and the game goes to the next round. If the picture is not good enough, the next place team is judged. For the next round, each person moves up one chair towards the head of the line so everyone will get a chance to play all of the positions. Be sure to have enough pictures that everyone will have a chance to be in all of the positions.

The teams may not ask questions about what is being drawn on their backs. They should also be encouraged not to look at the other teams to see what they are drawing. The pictures you choose to have them draw should be fairly simple. Some suggestions would be a star, house, flower, tree, boat, letter of the alphabet, happy face, sun, lightbulb, etc.

DISCUSSION IDEAS:
- What did you see happening during this activity?
- How did you feel when you were the person who started the drawing?
- How did you feel when you were in the middle of the line?
- How did you feel when you were the person drawing on the paper?
- What made this activity hard to accomplish?
- Why did the picture look different at the end than it did at the beginning?
- What would have made this activity easier to accomplish?
- What can this activity tell us about communication?
- What are some of the ways that the facts of a story get changed?
- What are some of the consequences of information being changed?
- Does it make any difference in the end whether the information was changed on purpose or by mistake?
- What steps can we take to be sure that information is not heard or told incorrectly?
- Whose job is it to be sure that information gets passed along correctly? The person doing the talking or the person doing the listening? Why?

BACK TO BACK DRAWING

TOPIC AREA: Communication

CONCEPT: For real communication to take place it is important to use good listening skills. These would be skills such as eye contact, body language, concentration, facial expression, etc. To really get your point across you need to utilize these skills in your conversations. When you do not use these skills, communication becomes difficult and understanding becomes impossible.

METHOD: Classroom Activity

TIME FRAME: 15 minutes plus discussion

MATERIALS NEEDED:
- A pencil for every two students
- A blank piece of paper for each student
- Two different pictures of various geometric shapes (two pictures for each pair of students)

ACTIVITY: Have each person in the class get with a partner. Have the partners sit back-to-back . There should be enough space between the pairs they can not see what another pair is drawing. Give one of the partners a pencil and a blank piece of paper. If possible, give them a hard surface to draw upon. Give the other partner a picture. Have them return to their partner and begin describing the picture to their partner while the partner tries to draw the picture they are describing. The person giving the instructions may not look at what their partner is drawing nor may the partner look at the picture that is being described. If you wish, you may let them ask questions of each other. If you are working with older kids or wish to repeat the exercise with a new picture, then you would not allow them to ask questions until the second round. Once the first person is done describing the picture and his partner has drawn it to the best of his ability, let them compare pictures. Now have them switch roles. Give the person who drew the first picture a new picture and he will now be the one giving instructions.

DISCUSSION IDEAS:
- How similar did your picture that you drew look to the picture that your partner was describing?
- What were some of the things that made it difficult to complete this activity?
- What were the feelings that you felt when you were the person describing the picture to your partner?
- Why did you feel this way?
- What were the feelings that you felt when you were the person trying to draw the picture from your partner's description?
- Why did you feel this way?
- How do you think this applies to communicating with others?
- Describe situations where you have felt this way with your friends.
- Describe situations where you have felt this way with your parents.
- What steps could you take to be sure that others do not feel this way when they are talking to you?
- What steps could you take if others made you feel this way when you were talking with them?

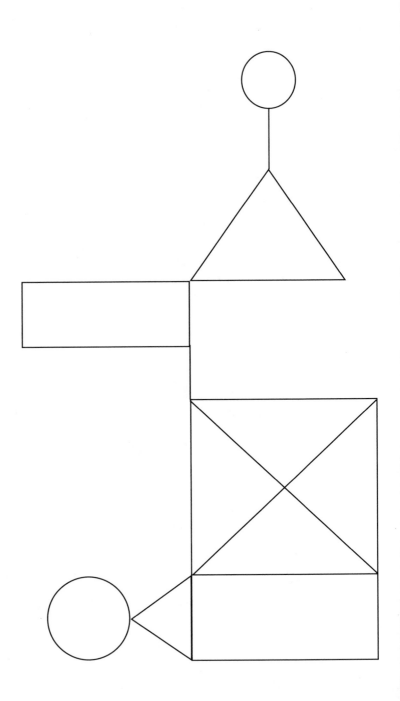

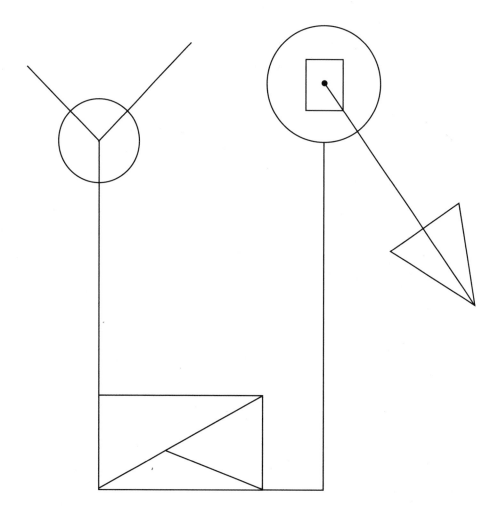

BAD VISION

TOPIC AREA: Alcohol

CONCEPT: There are numerous body functions that do not work as well when you are under the influence as they do when you are sober. One of these is your vision. When you are under the influence of alcohol, your vision becomes less acute. Blurry vision and poor night vision are two of the effects that you will experience. This is a real problem since most drinking occurs at night and then the person wants to drive his/her car home.

METHOD: Classroom Demonstration

TIME FRAME: 5 minutes plus discussion time

MATERIALS NEEDED:
- One pair of dark sunglasses
- Some Vaseline
- Three round balloons

ACTIVITY: Chose one person from your class to come up front. Blow up three round balloons. Give the balloons to the student one at a time and have him bounce them into the air. The object is to see if he can start with one balloon, then add the second balloon, then the third balloon and keep them all in the air at one time. He should be real successful with two balloons and somewhat successful with three. Now collect the balloons from him and tell the class that you are going to simulate one of the effects of being under the influence.

This effect is blurred and darkened vision. Give him the pair of sunglasses. Beforehand rub Vaseline on the front of the lenses. The Vaseline works best if it is rubbed on in a circular motion. Now have him repeat the same activity while wearing the Vaseline covered sunglasses.

VARIATION:

Instead of having only one person in front doing this activity, have three people. By having them all hitting balloons simultaneously, greater confusion occurs and the effect is more pronounced.

DISCUSSION IDEAS:

- How did the person do keeping the balloons in the air when he did not have the sunglasses on?
- How did the person do keeping the balloons in the air when he had the sunglasses on?
- What effects of being under the influence did the sunglasses simulate?
- List activities that would be impaired when you were under the influence.
- List jobs that would be dangerous if done by a person who was impaired by these effects.
- Would you want a person with these impairments to drive you home?
- What can we learn about the effects of alcohol from this activity?

BALLOON RACE

TOPIC AREAS: Alcohol, Other Drugs

CONCEPT: When you begin to experiment with alcohol and other drug use no one can be one hundred per cent sure of the effects they will have on your body. Some people are genetically predisposed to become addicted to drugs quicker than others. Some people have physiological problems that are not apparent until stress is put on them by certain drugs. Drugs have different effects on bodies at various levels of growth. Many times the younger the person, the greater the effect. The key idea here is that we can't tell each individual what the precise effect will be on his/her body from a drug. We can't even be sure what the drug really contains unless it has been analyzed by a laboratory.

METHOD: Classroom Activity

TIME FRAME: 10 minutes plus discussion time

MATERIALS NEEDED:
- One balloon for each person in the group (they should be of varying shapes and sizes)
- One roll of masking tape

ACTIVITY: Divide the group into teams of four or five. Give each person a balloon. The balloons should be various sizes and shapes. It doesn't matter which person gets what size or shape balloon nor how many of each size or shape balloon are given to each team. Draw a starting line on the floor with the masking tape. Have the teams line up in single file lines behind the masking tape. On your command the first person in line will blow their balloon up and release it in front of them. Their balloon will fly somewhere. Wherever their balloon lands, they are to run to that spot and stand. The next person in line runs to where they are standing, blows up their balloon and releases it in front of them. Wherever it lands, they are to run and stand at that spot. Then the next person on their team runs to them and blows up their balloon and releases it in front of them. This process continues until all of the members of the team have blown up their balloons and are standing where their balloon landed. Whichever team has a member the farthest from the starting line after the last person has released their balloon is the winner.

The game will go something like this. Some people will release their balloon and it will go straight out in front of them. Some will release their balloon and it will go in circles and land behind them. Others will find their balloon going straight down to the ground and staying there. All of the balloons will react in different ways. No one will be able to predict what direction, distance or path their balloon will take before they let it go. The team that wins, will do so because of luck not any great skill on their part.

DISCUSSION IDEAS:
* Did each team cover the same distance? Why not?
* Describe the different patterns the balloons made?
* What kind of control did you have over where or how far your balloon flew?
* What determined the direction and distance the balloon flew?
* Did the balloon always fly in a direction that was beneficial to your team?

- What could your team have done to improve their chances of winning?
- What can this activity teach us about the effects of alcohol and other drugs?
- Does each person react the same way to the same drug?
- What are some of the factors that might influence the way a person reacts to a drug?
- What control do you have over the ingredients that go into making illegal street drugs?
- How can you know for sure what is in each illegal street drug?
- What do the manufacturers of illegal street drugs do to make their drugs stretch farther and be more profitable?
- What impact will this "cutting" or mixing of the drug with other substances that are similar in color and texture to the drug have on the user?

BLIND LINE UP

TOPIC AREA: Communication

CONCEPT: This activity stresses the importance of working together and formulating a plan instead of everyone just going off and doing their own thing. The idea of how a leader is chosen and how a plan is put into operation can also be looked at.

METHOD: Classroom Activity

TIME FRAME: 10 to 15 minutes plus discussion time

MATERIALS NEEDED:
• One blindfold for each person

ACTIVITY: Divide your group into teams of about fifteen. Have the two groups separate themselves from each other. Instruct each person to sit down and put on their blindfolds. Stress the fact that if they want to get the full affect of this activity, they should be sure that they cannot see out from under their blindfolds. Explain that the object of this activity is for each team to form a single file line with the shortest person in front and the tallest person in the back. Depending on the age of the group you can allow them to talk while trying to line up, or to make it harder you can have them complete the activity in silence. Another way to make the activity more difficult is to not break them up into groups. The more people that have to form one line, the longer and harder the activity will be.

DISCUSSION IDEAS:

- How did you feel when I told you what the activity was going to be?
- How hard did you think this would be to accomplish? Why?
- Did any of you get lost during the activity? How did you find the group again?
- What problems did you have getting the line formed? Why?
- How did leadership emerge in the group? Were they chosen? Was it just the loudest person? Was it the pushiest person?
- How did the group know when you were done with the activity?
- What suggestions would you have for the group if we were to repeat this activity?
- What do you think this activity can tell us about communication?
- What skills of communication can this activity teach us?

BLIND WALK

TOPIC AREA: Communication

CONCEPT: As we communicate with each other, we need to rely on more than our verbal skills to do the job. Listening to both what is said and what is implied is important to good understanding. Sometimes for good communication to happen there needs to be a certain level of trust. This is the case when you are talking about something that is very personal to you; you would not expect what you have said to be shared with others.

METHOD: Classroom Activity

TIME FRAME: 30 minutes plus discussion time

MATERIALS NEEDED:
• One blindfold for every two participants

ACTIVITY: This activity is best done outside. Have your group break up into partners. Explain to them the hazards of this activity and stress the importance of safety and taking personal responsibility. Anyone who does not take personal responsibility or acts in an unsafe manner is to be immediately eliminated from the activity. It is strongly recommended that you have two or three people help you keep this activity a safe one. Their job will be to keep people from straying off the course. The activity starts with one of the pair blindfolded. The other person is the leader. You or your designated person will lead the group around a course of your own design. The course should not be too difficult, but there should be sufficient obstacles to create a challenge for your age group. The length of the course should be about five minutes. The group should walk in a line with the sighted person keeping the blindfolded person on the course and safe. They may talk as much as they want during this part of the activity. After a period of time, have the partners switch places and continue walking. Remind your class that if they cheat and peek out from under their blindfolds, most of the affect of the activity will be lost.

After both people have had a chance to experience the activity, it is time to take it one step further. You will repeat the exercise, except this time there will be no talking or sounds of any kind allowed during the walk. If you would like, you can have them switch partners at this point. Give everyone a chance to figure out what kinds of signals they are going to use to tell the blindfolded person they have to turn, step up or down, bend down and walk under something, etc. Since they can't use sounds, they must develop another system of communication. Remind them that once they start there are to be no sounds of any kind. Once again have them switch roles so both partners experience the activity. During the switch over, allow them to talk and decide on the same or new signals. Anytime the group gets too spread out on your walk, stop and wait for them to close the line back up. Do not allow them to remove their blindfolds or talk during these stops.

DISCUSSION IDEAS:
- How did you feel during the first walk when you were the blindfolded person?
- How did you feel during the first walk when you were the leader?

- Did you feel safe in the hands of your leader? Why or why not?
- What kinds of things did your partner do to make you feel safe or scared?
- Were you able to follow your leader without any problems? Why or why not?
- As the leader, did you have any problems getting your partner to follow? Why or why not?
- In the second activity, how did you feel when you were blindfolded?
- In the second activity, how did you feel as the leader?
- What signals did you use to guide your partner when you couldn't talk?
- How well did these signals work? Did you change them when you switched?
- Did you as the blindfolded person listen harder when your partner was using his voice or when he was using signals? Why?
- Did you as the leader have to work harder when you were using your voice or when you were using signals? Why?
- How can this activity help us to improve our communication skills?
- What kinds of things can we do to improve our communication?
- What role did trust play in this activity?
- What role does trust play in our communications with others?
- How can we establish that trust with others?
- What kinds of things break down our trust in others?
- What would we have to do to reestablish that trust again?
- Is this process any different when we deal with our friends as opposed to when we deal with our parents?

BODY SHUFFLE

TOPIC AREAS: Communication, Decision Making, Problem Solving

CONCEPT: When a group has to decide on an action, how is the decision made? The group dynamics that take place are important for kids to know. One area that we deal very little with is how to influence a group decision, yet this is the setting in which most kids get in trouble. This activity will allow us to look at areas such as working together, making group decisions and communicating in a group setting.

METHOD: Classroom Activity

TIME FRAME: 15 minutes per two teams, plus discussion time

MATERIALS NEEDED:
* A long, narrow structure (about 25 to 30 feet) that can accommodate twelve to sixteen kids standing single file on it at one time. Good examples would be two by four pieces of lumber, a low wall or a long log. If you use two by fours, it is more challenging to place them on cinder blocks to make the event more challenging. You will need one of these structures for every twelve to sixteen people in your group.

ACTIVITY: Divide your group into teams of six to eight people. Have two teams stand on top of your structure. They will naturally be in a single file line. Have the two teams face each other. This is not a competition. The object is for all the people from one team to exchange places with the people on the other team without stepping off of the structure. The two teams will reform their lines with the person that was in the middle, now being on the far end away from where his team started. The last person on the team will end up in the middle, but on the opposite side from where his team started. Once you begin they can not step off of the structure and onto the ground. If a person's foot or any other part of his body hits the ground, that person must return to the place on the log from where he started. This is an activity that requires a lot of group cooperation and discussion among each other as to the best way to accomplish the goal.

I would not have the teams any larger than six to eight or the activity will take too long. If your total group is larger than the twelve to sixteen, you have a couple of options: You can have enough structures for everyone or you can rotate the groups on the structure so that they take turns. If you have them take turns on the structure, do not let the waiting team watch the activity or they will benefit from the first team's mistakes. This is a frustrating activity for some groups because they will have it almost accomplished when someone will fall off and have to return to their original spot. If that is true with your group, be sure to discuss frustration and the feelings that come from that frustration. These same feelings might be found in making a group decision that could be harmful or dangerous to you.

DISCUSSION IDEAS:
* How did you decide what the procedure would be used to pass people along the structure?

- Did a leader emerge among the group? How did this happen?
- Was more than one way tried to see what would work best to pass people along the structure?
- Which ways were chosen and how were they decided upon?
- How did you feel when you fell off of the structure and had to start again?
- How did you feel when someone else on the team fell and had to start again?
- Did everyone play an equal role in deciding how the passing was going to be done?
- Did everyone care about how the people were to be passed?
- What can this activity tell us about communication?
- What can this activity tell us about group decision making?

BRIDGES

TOPIC AREAS: Decision Making, Problem Solving

CONCEPT: Many times, when given a problem to solve, there is more than one solution. This is true whether the problem is being solved by an individual or by a group of people. However when the problem is being worked on by more than one person, the number of solutions and the methods to get to those solutions become increasingly greater. Kids need to have experience in group problem solving and working together. This is the format they will more than likely encounter in the typical workplace. Without an understanding of group dynamics, opinion persuasion, idea presentation and individual follow through, they may not succeed in the average workplace environment.

METHOD: Classroom Activity

TIME FRAME: 30 minutes plus discussion time

MATERIALS NEEDED:
- A large stack of newspapers per team of five people
- One or two rolls of masking tape per each team of five people
- One large can (grapefruit juice or beef stew size, contents are to be left in the can)

ACTIVITY: Divide your group into teams of five. Give each team a stack of newspapers and two rolls of masking tape. The assignment is to build a bridge that is high enough that the can will be able to pass under it in an upright position and strong enough that the can will be able to sit on it. They may only use newspapers and masking tape to build the bridge. If they need more newspaper or masking tape, you may supply them from a central supply. They may not attach, lean, or in any other way use additional supports for their bridge. Give them a time limit for building. Twenty minutes seems to be adequate, but this is flexible according to the needs of your group. Be sure to give them time warnings throughout the activity so they will know how much time they have left. When time is over, take the can around to each bridge and see if it will fit under the bridge and if the bridge can support the weight of the can. This is not a contest. Each group has the same chance of being successful.

DISCUSSION IDEAS:
- What was your reaction when you first heard you had to build a bridge out of newspaper that would hold a heavy can?
- What planning did your group do before it started building?
- Did the plan work or were adjustments necessary during the building?
- What kind of adjustments needed to be made?
- Why were adjustments necessary? Were they successful?
- What type of leadership did your group have?
- How was the leader chosen?
- How did you feel towards your leader?
- How was the building plan decided upon?
- Did everyone have the same amount of input into deciding how the bridge would be built? Why or why not?

- How were jobs divided among the group?
- Were some people harder workers than others?
- How did you feel towards those that weren't contributing very much?
- How did your group deal with opposing points of view as to how the bridge should be built?
- How did your group deal with frustration?
- Describe a project in the past where you have worked with others.
- Why do you think it is important to know how to work with others?
- What are some behaviors that are important when working with others?

BUILDING WHAT YOU HEAR

TOPIC: Communication

CONCEPT: When information is passed from one person to the next, things can become confused and distorted. This is especially true when we are in a hurry or we don't know the whole story. If we are in a hurry, we leave out important facts. If we don't know the whole story, we may fill in the blanks with information that may or may not be true. Either way, the story becomes farther and farther from the truth. If someone wants to know the truth, they need to go to the original source and find out what they want to know. We should never completely believe anyone who is relating information to us second or third hand unless we can verify the information in some manner.

METHOD: Classroom Activity

TIME FRAME: 30 minutes plus discussion time

MATERIALS NEEDED:
- Twenty multi-colored miniature marshmallows for every three people in the class
- Twenty multi-colored toothpicks for every three people in the class
- A lunch sack or plastic baggie for each team of three

ACTIVITY: Divide your group into teams of three. Have each team create a design using up to ten various colored toothpicks and up to ten various colored marshmallows. The designs must lay flat on the table or floor.

The design should be two dimensional rather than three dimensional. As the teams are creating their design, they need to set aside the same number and color of marshmallows and toothpicks they used to build their design. Have them put these into a small sack. This set of marshmallows and toothpicks will be given to the builder on the team that must recreate that particular design so he will have the right materials to work with. Once all the teams have created a design, explain that each team must designate an explainer, a messenger and a builder. Separate the explainer, messenger and builder. At this point have the explainers go and sit by a different team's design. Do not let any other member of the team see this design. Send the builders to the other end of the room and give them the sack of marshmallows and toothpicks that corresponds with those from the design where the explainer is now sitting. Have the builders sit facing away from the explainers so they can not see the design that they will have to build.

The activity can now begin. The messenger goes down by the explainer. Have the explainer positioned so that the messenger cannot see the design. The explainer will tell the messenger what the structure looks like. Then the messenger goes down to where the builder is located and without being able to see what the builder is building, he relays what the explainer has told him him about the design. The messenger may make as many trips back and forth between the explainer and the builder, to get instructions or ask questions, as he wishes. At no time may the messenger see the actual design the explainer has in front of him or the design the builder is building. Questions may be asked, but looking is not allowed. When each team has finished recreating the design they have been assigned, have the entire team get together and see how closely they were able to duplicate the original by using only verbal instructions.

VARIATIONS:
You may use more than one messenger. This helps the activity end quicker. It is also a good idea with younger groups. They can transfer the information faster and in smaller chunks.

Do not have the correct colored toothpicks and marshmallows put into a sack for each team. Simply place a pile of toothpicks and marshmallows out on a table and have the builders find what they were told to use.

To make the activity more challenging, you may allow them to build three dimensional structures that have to be duplicated rather than two dimensional structures.

DISCUSSION IDEAS:
• What took place during this activity?
• What were you thinking when you were creating the designs?
• Were some of the designs harder to recreate than others? Why?
• What were some of the problems the explainer had?
• What were some of the problems the messenger had?
• What were some of the problems the builder had?
• Which position do you feel was the most difficult? Why?
• Which position do you feel was the easiest? Why?
• Which position was the most important? Why?

- What kinds of things did the messenger have to do to be sure he heard the instructions properly?
- What kinds of things did the messenger have to do to be sure that the builder heard him correctly?
- Why is listening such an important part of this activity?
- How can we relate this activity to communication?
- Have you or someone you know ever had a situation where someone told something about you and didn't tell the whole story? Describe some of these situations.
- Have you ever heard gossip that you knew wasn't true?
- How do you stop gossip once it gets started?
- What are some listening skills that will help keep the story clear?
- What are some of the behaviors that get in the way of us clearly understanding something that someone else is telling us?
- How can these behaviors be corrected?
- Which person is more important, the person telling the story or the person listening to the story? Why?

CHOICES AND CONSEQUENCES

TOPIC AREA: Decision Making

CONCEPT: Many of our youth have blinders on when it comes to making a decision. They look at one, maybe two alternatives and make their choice from those. Many times the consequences of their choices are not even considered when making a decision. We need to educate our youth to consider all of the alternatives and the consequences before making a decision. By looking at all of the possible consequences, hopefully they will consider the impact on their lives of certain choices *before* engaging in behavior which may bring negative consequences.

METHOD: Classroom Demonstration

TIME FRAME: 5 minutes plus discussion time

MATERIALS NEEDED:
- A small piece of paper for each student
- A pen or pencil for each student

ACTIVITY: Draw the following diagram on the board. Do not let the students see you drawing. Cover up the drawing until you are ready to start the activity.

After unveiling the drawing to the students, ask them to spend a couple of minutes counting the number of squares they see. Have them write their answers on a small piece of paper and collect them. Just to let you know, I have counted as many as thirty. Your students

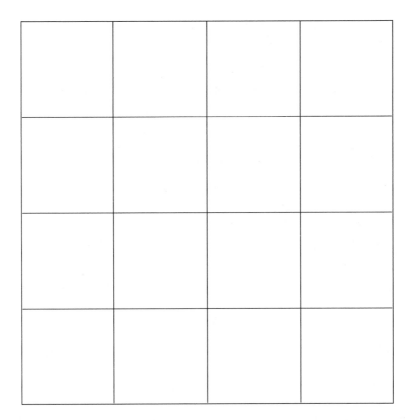

will probably guess anywhere from sixteen to thirty. Write the various answers on the board. Now show them the correct number of squares.

DISCUSSION IDEAS:
- How many squares did you see immediately?
- How many squares did you see after you had studied the diagram for awhile?
- Why did you keep discovering more squares?
- Describe some situations where you would have to make a decision.
- List all of the alternatives and the consequences for these choices.

- Are consequences always bad?
- What happens when we do not look at all of the consequences?
- Who can we turn to help us explore our alternatives?
- Who should have the final decision as to which alternative we choose? Why?
- Who is responsible for the decisions that you make?
- What comes first, a decision or an action? What impact could this have on the decisions we make and the actions we take?
- How can we apply this activity to alcohol and drug use?

CILIA VOLLEYBALL

TOPIC AREA: Tobacco

CONCEPT: Inside the airway passage that leads to the lungs, is a system that protects the lungs from small particles of smoke and ash. This system is made up of fine hairs which line the air passage and are called cilia. These cilia wave back and forth and trap the small particles as they pass by on their way to the lungs. These hairlike fingers then work the particles back up to the mouth through the use of mucus and keep the particles from settling in the lungs. When a person smokes, the tar from the cigarette is inhaled and deposited on the cilia. Soon the cilia become covered with tar and can no longer perform their waving action and are not effective in trapping the particles. When the waving action ceases, the tar continues through the passageway and becomes deposited in the lungs. Over a period of time the cilia cease to function altogether and the body produces extra mucus to try to protect the lungs. This extra mucus builds up in the lungs and has to be coughed out by the smoker. This is the basis for "smoker's cough".

METHOD: Classroom Activity

TIME FRAME: 20 minutes plus discussion time

MATERIALS NEEDED:
- 10 volleyball-size balloons
- A rope to serve as a net.

ACTIVITY: Divide your class into two teams. Stretch a rope, which will serve as the net, about three feet off the ground across the room and have the two teams lie down on their backs with their heads towards the net. This activity is played much like a volleyball game. There are a few differences. No one may get up off of the floor. They must always have their heads towards the net. Instead of having a server, the teacher or their appointee throws a balloon onto one side of the net. The team must hit the balloon at least three times before it may pass over the net. When a team can't return the balloon, then a point is awarded to the other team. Teams rotate positions just as they would in regular volleyball so that everyone gets to play the different positions. To make the game more exciting, you may have more than one balloon in play at a time.

This activity simulates the action of the cilia. The balloons represent particles of smoke or tar that pass down the airway. The arms of the players represent the cilia. After playing the game for a while, stop and explain this to the students. To simulate the problem of cilia becoming covered with tar, have some students use only one arm to hit the balloons, with the other arm kept out of play completely. This portrays the cilia becoming covered with tar and ceasing to catch particles. You may have some students who can't hit the balloons once they have had a turn. This further inhibits the team's abilities to keep the balloon in the air. Any penalty or combination that causes fewer arms to be used will demonstrate your point of diminished cilia effectiveness.

DISCUSSION IDEAS:
• In the beginning was this game hard to play?

- As we continued the game did it become harder? Why?
- What can this activity tell us about smoking?
- What do you think having more than one balloon going at a time could tell us about smoking?
- How did you feel when your team couldn't use all of their arms to hit the balloon?
- When many people weren't using their arms, what problems did you have?
- How can we relate those problems to smoking?
- Using the game as an example, how well does your body's defense system work when the cilia become covered with tar?
- When some people couldn't hit the balloons, what did others have to do to compensate for them?
- What does your body do when some of its cilia are not being effective?

CIRCLE JUGGLE

TOPIC AREAS: Alcohol, Other Drugs, Stress

CONCEPT: There are situations in life that become frustrating when you add additional stressors to them. In managing stress, you have to understand that the more complicated the issue becomes, the more stress you will be under. You can also use this activity to show that sometimes drug impairment does not show up until you get in a situation that demands a great deal of concentration. Some drunk drivers have found that they can drive slowly, and with extreme concentration, manage to stay on the road. But if any emergency or fast reaction situation arises, they will have trouble reacting in time.

METHOD: Classroom Activity

TIME FRAME: 20 minutes per topic area, plus discussion time

MATERIALS NEEDED:
- Five tennis balls for each group of ten to twelve students.
- Two different sized balls for each group of ten to twelve students

ACTIVITY: Divide your class into smaller groups of ten to twelve people. Have each group form a circle approximately fifteen to twenty feet in diameter. Designate one person in each group as the leader. Give this person one tennis ball. Have all of the other members of the group raise their hand. The leader then gently tosses the tennis ball underhand to another person in the group making sure that the person is somewhere across the circle from him. He may not toss the ball to the person directly on either side of him. When each person has the ball thrown to him, he puts his hand down making it clear to the rest of the group that he has already received the ball. That person then tosses the ball to someone else in the circle that still has his hand up and is not on either side of him. This procedure continues until everyone has had the ball tossed to him. The last person tosses the ball back to the leader. The purpose of this first round is to establish a pattern. With that in mind, each person must remember who tossed the ball to him and who he tossed the ball to. After the pattern has been established practice going through the exact same pattern a couple of times so that everyone will be able to remember exactly who tossed the ball to him and to whom he tosses the ball. If you would like, have the teams race against each other a couple of times to see which team can get the ball through the pattern first.

STRESS: Start with one ball being tossed around the circle, then add a second ball. To do this, give the leader both tennis balls and tell him that after he starts tossing the first ball around the circle,he is to then start the second ball also. After they have tried two balls, then have them try three, four and five.

DISCUSSION IDEAS FOR STRESS:
- How hard was it for you when there was only one ball being tossed around?
- What happened when an additional ball was added?

- What happened as more balls were added to the circle?
- How did you feel when only one ball was being tossed around the circle?
- How did your feelings change as more balls were added to the circle?
- How could we relate this to stress in our lives?
- How hard is it to handle a small amount of stress in our lives?
- How hard is it to handle many different areas of stress at one time in our lives?
- What are some examples of stress that you could have in your life?
- What are some of the ways that we handle stress in our lives?
- Are all the methods for handling stress beneficial to us?
- What are some of the harmful ways that people handle stress?

ALCOHOL OR DRUG IMPAIRMENT: Use the above activities with this added variation. Introduce two other balls that are a completely different size than the ones being tossed around. These balls are not to be tossed across the circle, but are to be passed in opposite directions from person to person, hand to hand around the circle.

The activity that uses the five balls being tossed can help you show that when you are under the influence, it becomes harder and harder to continue performing at the same level as before. The different sized balls being passed around can be the situation or emergency that occurs and you have trouble handling it because of your impairment. The balls being passed around will end up in the hands of someone at the same time they are being tossed a tennis ball . This activity is easily related to driving while under the influence. One major concern for the drinking driver is being able to do more than one thing at once. This concept is called tracking.

DISCUSSION IDEAS FOR IMPAIRMENT:
* How did you feel when only one ball was being tossed around?
* How did you feel as more and more balls were added to the circle?
* Were you able to perform as well when there were five balls being tossed? Why or why not?
* How did you feel when the different sized ball was being passed around?
* Did you have any control over when the different sized ball was passed to you? How does this relate to drinking and driving?
* How can we relate this entire activity to drinking and driving?

CIRCLE JUGGLE WITH A GOAL

TOPIC AREA: Goal Setting

CONCEPT: It is much easier to reach your goals when they are clearly defined. There can be many things going on in your life, but a clearly defined goal will help you focus your energies on what is really important to you. However, sometimes no matter how much concentration you have, or planning that you have done, things over which you have no control, can go wrong. When this happens, as will be demonstrated by the object which is passed around the circle during the activity, your students must be ready to do some rethinking rather than abandon their goals altogether. Having no clearly defined goals is a factor in preventing drug use and other anti-social behaviors. If you are working on a goal, then you have less chance of becoming side tracked by poor decisions that will hurt your chances of achieving your goals.

METHOD: Classroom Activity

TIME FRAME: 20 minutes plus discussion time

MATERIALS NEEDED:
- Five tennis balls for each group of ten to twelve students.
- One different colored ball for each group of ten to twelve students
- Two different sized balls for each group of ten to twelve students

ACTIVITY: Divide your class into groups of ten to twelve people. Have each group form a circle approximately fifteen to twenty feet in diameter. Designate one person in each group as the leader. Give this person one tennis ball. Have all of the other members of the group raise their hand. The leader then gently tosses the tennis ball underhand to another person in the group. That person must be somewhere across the circle from him; the leader, nor anyone else, may toss the ball to the person directly on either side. When each person has the ball thrown to him, he puts his hand down making it clear to the rest of the group that he has already received the ball. He then tosses the ball to someone else in the circle that still has his hand up and is not on either side of him. This procedure continues until everyone has had the ball tossed to him. The last person tosses the ball back to the leader. The purpose of this first round is to establish a pattern. With that in mind, each person must remember who tossed the ball to him and to whom he tossed the ball. After the pattern has been established practice going through the exact same pattern a couple of times so that everyone will be able to remember exactly who tossed the ball to him and to whom he tosses the ball. If you would like, have the teams race against each other a couple of times to see which team can get the ball through the pattern first.

You are now ready to start adding more tennis balls to the pattern. Have the group repeat the pattern with two tennis balls. Then add a third tennis ball and see how they do. Now add a fourth tennis ball and finally add a fifth tennis ball to the pattern. They should complete the pattern with two tennis balls before you have them stop and then introduce the third tennis ball.

Continue this procedure until all five tennis balls have been successfully added.

Repeat the same activity listed above except this time, when you have already somewhat mastered having five balls being tossed around the circle, stop and add a new ball. Explain to the group that you are going to substitute a ball of a different color into the activity. Instead of a tennis ball being tossed around as ball number four, you will have the leader toss a ball of a different color. Tell the groups that you don't care what happens to the tennis balls as they are being tossed around the circle, but you want them to be sure that the colored ball is not dropped. Tell the leader of each group that as he tosses the colored ball, everyone should be warned that it is coming by saying "special ball" as he tosses.

After they have tried and completed this procedure, introduce two other balls that are completely different sizes than the ones being tossed back and forth. These balls are not to be tossed across the circle, but are to be passed in opposite directions, from person-to-person hand-to-hand around the circle.

The concepts that are being shown here are these: The colored ball represents your goal. When you are aware of what you want to accomplish, you are more likely to concentrate on the actions that will help you reach your goal. As the colored ball is tossed around the circle, the kids will concentrate harder on it than the regular tennis balls - the colored ball will be dropped fewer times than the regular tennis balls. The second concept has to do with the different sized ball that is being passed around the circle from person to person.

The idea is that when a person has the tennis ball being thrown to him at the same time that he has been passed the different sized ball, he will have a hard time holding on to both of them. The different sized ball represents an unexpected event in your life that you have no control over but makes it so that you have to change or cancel your goal. An example would be the track athlete who worked hard for four years to make the Olympic Team, only to be injured the day before the qualifying trials.

DISCUSSION IDEAS:
- How did you feel when there was only one ball being tossed around?
- How did you feel as more and more balls were added to the activity?
- Did you find the colored ball easier or harder to catch? Why?
- Did you concentrate harder when it was your turn to catch or toss the colored ball? Why?
- How can we relate this activity to goal setting?
- What are some of the goals that you might have at this age?
- What makes it hard to accomplish a goal?
- How did you feel when the different size ball was added to the activity?
- What are some of the unexpected events that could have an impact on a person's goal?
- How should we react to an unexpected event in the area of goal setting?

CONNECTIONS

TOPIC AREAS: Alcohol, Other Drugs

CONCEPT: When you are under the influence of a drug from the depressant family, you will have slowed reaction time. Part of this impairment comes from the structure and behavior of the brain. When you want to send messages across the brain, these messages are transmitted via electrical impulses across the synapse by a substance called the nuerotransmitter. When you are under the influence of a depressant drug, this process of transmitting the information across the synapse is slowed down. This will slow down the speed in which your brain can respond to changing situations.

METHOD: Classroom Demonstration

TIME FRAME: 10 Minutes plus discussion time

MATERIALS NEEDED: None

ACTIVITY: Have twelve people come to the front of the room. Have them line up in a single file line facing the class. Place yourself in the middle of the line, also facing the class. Have all of the people hold hands. If this is too disruptive in your group, then have them grab the arm of the person next to them. Tell them that you will squeeze the person's hand that is on either side of you at the same time. They will in turn squeeze the person next to them and so on down the line until the last person in line feels the squeeze. The last person in line is to raise his free hand when the squeeze is felt. This is a race, so each team needs to go as fast as they can. Practice this a couple of times with the two teams. Now do it three times for real. Have the class judge which team wins each race.

When you have found the fastest team, indicate that for the next race you are going to make that team drunk. The way to do this is to have that team hold their hands up at shoulder height, like they were being mugged and someone has said "Stick 'em up". This time when this team sends their message they will do so by opening and closing each of their hands individually. The hands are still being held at shoulder height so that the class can see them open and close as the message is passed down the line. The other team is still connected by holding hands and will continue to pass the message by squeezing hands. The leader will hold the hand of the first person on each team. When the first person on the team holding hands feels you squeeze their hand they will pass the message by squeezing the hand that they are holding. The other team will pass the message by opening and closing their hands one at a time, then the next person in line will open and close first one of their hands and then the other hand. The message is passed down the line in this fashion from person to person. Obviously the team that is still holding hands will be able to pass the message down the line faster than the team that has their hands at shoulder height. You have just demonstrated both conditions of the brain. The one holding hands has its neurotransmitters firing correctly and the other brain has their process slowed by drugs.

DISCUSSION IDEAS:
* What happened when both teams were holding hands?

- What happened when only one team was holding hands?
- What caused the one team to be so slow in the second part of the activity?
- What can this activity tell us about depressant drugs and the brain?
- What can this activity tell us about depressant drugs and reaction time?
- What happens when an emergency situation comes up and the brain is impaired by a depressant drug?
- What are some of the activities that you are involved in where this impairment would jeopardize your performance?
- What kinds of jobs would be dangerous with this type of impairment?

COPY CAT

TOPIC AREA: Goal Setting

CONCEPT: When we start to talk about goals, we have to realize that the only goals our students will follow through with are goals that are beneficial to them. If it is an imposed goal, they will not work very hard to achieve it. As a teacher, parent or significant other we may think that we know what is best for our kids, but until they feel the same way, we will not get the commitment we want. A prime example is a behavior change that we feel would be beneficial for the individual. We can tell them all we want that we feel it is good for them, but until the change is something they want, it will not take place. So when talking about goal setting, be sure the goals are ones chosen by the student, not imposed by someone else.

METHOD: Classroom Activity

TIME FRAME: 5 minutes plus discussion time

MATERIALS NEEDED: None

ACTIVITY: Have everyone in your group choose a partner. Have them stand face to face with their partner. Choose the shortest of each pair to be the leader. Have them both raise their hands up in front of their chest and hold them like they were going to play "patty cake". The hands should be facing each other about six inches apart. On your command, the leader is to move his hands and allow the other person to follow his hand motions with their hands. Let this continue for about a minute. Now have the partners reverse roles and the taller of the two is the leader. Allow this to continue for about a minute. Stop the activity. Do not admonish those who are not going slow enough for their partner to follow them. This is natural and is part of the learning activity.

DISCUSSION IDEAS:
- How did you feel when you were the leader?
- How did you feel when you were the follower?
- Were you able to follow your partner's hands? Why or why not?
- How hard is it to follow someone else? Why?
- How can this activity help us to understand goal setting?
- Who should be the one that sets your goals? Why?
- Can you try to follow goals set by someone else?
- How hard do you work when someone else has set a goal for you?
- How hard do you work when you set your own goals?
- In what areas of life do other people set goals for us?
- In what areas of life do we set our own goals?
- In some areas of our life, does it matter who sets our goals? What areas would these be?
- What are some of the goals that our society has in common for all of us?

DECIDE EARLY

TOPIC AREA: Peer Pressure

CONCEPT: Research has found that those who make a decision not to use a substance before being asked, have a much better chance of resisting than do those who wait to make a decision until they are confronted with the choice. The early decision means they have already thought through the reasons not to use and are comfortable with that decision. Now all they have to do is be able to resist the situation they are in, not the decision of whether or not to use. Help your students make that early decision and have enough reasons not to use that they won't give in under pressure.

METHOD: Classroom Activity

TIME FRAME: 7 minutes plus discussion

MATERIALS NEEDED: None

ACTIVITY: Pair your group into partners. Have the partners face each other. Have them put their hands behind their back and extend any number of fingers on one or both hands. On the count of three, both partners are to bring their hands out in front of them and hold them chest high. The first of the two people who correctly adds up the number of fingers extended on his own hands and the hands of his partner yells out the answer. Remind them that it is the total number of fingers extended on all four hands that we are looking for. Have them go through this activity a couple of times with their partner and then have everyone switch to a new partner. Repeat the entire process through about three different partners. The key to winning this activity is to already know how many fingers you have extended on your own hands, so that when your partner's hands are brought out all you have to do is add his finger total to yours. This is the same theory as the early decision. When you already know what you are going to do, it is easier to respond when someone asks you to participate in a new behavior.

DISCUSSION IDEAS:
- How did you do on this activity?
- What strategy did you use to try to beat your partner?
- Did your strategy work? Why or why not?
- What do you think was the best strategy? Why?
- As you moved around the room, did others have a different strategy from yours or the partner you had been with? What was it?
- How do you think this activity can be useful in resisting peer pressure?
- When playing the game, did counting your own fingers help you win?
- Did you feel any pressure when the hands went up and the other person showed his fingers?
- Did you become frustrated during the activity? Why?
- Do you think making an early decision would help you resist peer pressure? Why or why not?
- Think about a situation where you had a hard time making up your mind about something. Describe the situation.
- How did you finally make your decision?

- What did you base your decision on?
- Do you think that same process would work with your decision about drug use? Why or why not?

DOLLAR BILL JUMP

TOPIC AREAS: Alcohol, Other Drugs

CONCEPT: When you are under the influence of some drugs, you have the belief that you can accomplish certain tasks when in reality you can't. This activity sounds so easy that everyone thinks they could do it. However, when they try, they find the task to be impossible for most and tough for all.

METHOD: Classroom Demonstration or Classroom Activity

TIME FRAME: 5 minutes plus discussion time

MATERIALS NEEDED:
- For Classroom Demonstration - A dollar bill
- For Classroom Activity - A roll of masking tape

ACTIVITY: For the classroom demonstration choose one person to come up in front of the class. Place the dollar bill down on the floor, extending the long way, right in front of his feet. Tell him to reach down (he does not have to keep his legs straight) and grab onto his toes and jump over the dollar bill. He can not let go of his toes when he does this. This is almost impossible for anyone to do. Give him a couple of tries. It looks so easy that he will have a hard time believing he can't do it. For the classroom activity place two lines of masking tape on the floor. Have them the same distance apart that a dollar bill would be. Now you can have the entire class line up on one side and give the jump a try. You may have them try one at a time or the entire group at once.

DISCUSSION IDEAS:

- How hard hard does this activity look?
- How did you feel when you gave it a try?
- What can this activity tell us about alcohol or drug impairment?
- Does the person who is impaired know that he can't do certain activities like drive a car?
- What is he thinking as he gets behind the wheel of the car?
- How good is our judgment working when we are impaired?
- Would we do things while impaired that normally we would not do?
- What kinds of things might we do that could result in trouble?
- How can we help a friend when he is impaired but doesn't know it?

FOUR ON A STRING

TOPIC AREA: Communication

CONCEPT: In our busy world, we have to communicate with more than one person at a time. We have multiple relationships that we are dealing with. It would be nice if we could just concentrate on one interaction at a time, but the reality is that we can't. We need to be able to balance our relationships and be able to shift our attention as the needs shift.

METHOD: Classroom Activity

TIME FRAME: 30 minutes plus discussion time

MATERIALS NEEDED:
- One eight foot length of string or rope per every four people
- Three blindfolds per every four people

ACTIVITY: Divide your class into groups of four people. Give each group an eight foot string or rope and three blindfolds. Explain to them the hazards of this activity and stress the importance of safety. Explain that each person must take personal responsibility for their actions and act in a safe manner. If anyone does not do this, then he should immediately be removed from the activity. It is strongly recommended that you have two or three people to help you keep this activity a safe one. Their job will be to keep people from straying off course. The activity starts with three people in the group putting their blindfolds on. Have the group of four line up single file with the non-blindfolded member third in line. All four people grab on to the rope or string. They may all be on the same side or different sides. It is easier if they are all on the same side. They are not to let go of the rope or string at any time during the activity.

The object is for the third person in line to lead the group through the course. You or your designated leader should be in front showing them the course. The groups should go through the course single file by fours following you or your designated leader. Do not let them choose their own course or stray from the one that you have indicated for them to follow. This becomes a safety concern. The course should be hard enough to challenge your age group. You might have them go under trees, around a car, under a jungle gym, walk over a log or through a gate. Just be sure that there are plenty of twists and turns that have to be negotiated during the walk. Judge for yourself the amount of time each person should lead. Five minutes is an average time for each leader. The non-blindfolded person will give verbal commands to his group as they negotiate the course. No one may talk but the leader. This rule may be altered depending on the age of your group. No one may touch anything but the string or rope. There will be obvious problems for the leader. He will have people in front of him that are difficult to control due to the distance, and he will have a person behind him that he might forget all about due to the challenges that he sees up front. Remind your class that if they cheat and peek out from under their blindfolds, some of the affect of the activity will be lost. After about five minutes, rotate each group's line so that everyone in the group will get a chance to experience each of the four positions in the line.

Be sure to stress safety before this activity. Remove anyone who is behaving in an unsafe manner.

DISCUSSION IDEAS:

- How did you feel when you were the first person in line?
- How did you feel when you were the second person in line?
- How did you feel when you were the leader?
- How did you feel when you were the last person in line?
- As the leader what problems did you encounter?
- As the last person in line did you ever feel forgotten by the leader?
- How safe did you feel during this activity?
- What was the hardest part of this activity? Why?
- As the leader, how much in control of the group did you feel?
- How clear were the instructions that the leader gave?
- What can this activity teach us about communication?
- Describe a situation where you felt that you were dealing with too many people at once.
- Describe a situation where you felt no one was in control.
- How can we be sure that our communication is clear and easily understood?
- What kinds of questions should we ask of a person when they are telling us something?
- As we increase the number of people we deal with does communication become harder? Why or why not?

FROGMAN

TOPIC AREA: Addiction

CONCEPT: When you are out of breath and you need to take another one there is no question that you will. You don't sit around thinking about it nor do you delay doing so. An addiction is very similar! You must have whatever it is that you are addicted to. We have watered down the concept of addiction by using phrases such as Choc-o-holic or "I need a soda pop or I'll die". Kids need to know that an addiction can take control over their body and dictate their behavior. The addiction will cause you to do things you normally wouldn't do, just to satisfy the addiction.

Everyone does not become addicted at the same rate. Some people are genetically predisposed to certain kinds of addiction. If your parents or grandparents were alcoholics, then your chances of becoming an alcoholic are greater. The length of time needed to become an alcoholic is also reduced. Kids become addicted faster than adults because their bodies have not matured physically yet. Different drugs can also cause you to become addicted faster than others.

METHOD: Classroom activity

TIME FRAME: 5 minutes plus discussion time

MATERIALS NEEDED: None

ACITIVITY: The object of the activity is to have the students see how long they can hold their breath. Have everyone stand up. Have them breath deeply a couple of times. Take air in slowly and let it out slowly. Now explain that you will count to three. When you reach three everyone is to take a deep breath and hold it for as long as they can. When they need to take a second breath, they are to sit down in their seats. Caution them to not hold their breath so long that they feel faint or are ready to pass out.

DISCUSSION IDEAS:
- Could you have held your breath for just a little longer than you did? Why not?
- Could you have held your breath for another three minutes?
- What would you have done if necessary to get a breath of air?
- Did everyone sit down and need a second breath at the same time?
- Why do you think some people could hold their breath longer than others?
- Do you think that all drugs are addicting at the same rate?
- What are some of the factors that make some people become addicted faster than other people?

GORILLA GAME

TOPIC AREA: Peer Pressure

CONCEPT: There are many ways to say "no" to an activity that a person feels is harmful or dangerous. We need to teach our kids that there is more than one way to say "no" and they need to look at them all and choose the one that feels right or works for them. Different situations may call for different approaches to saying "no", so they should not lock themselves into just one approach. After this activity, you will discuss why they chose the hand motion that they did. The concept for them to understand is that the hand motion they chose was what felt comfortable for them. This is the same concept behind saying "no". There are many ways to say "no", so choose what feels comfortable for you and use it. The more comfortable you are in saying "no" the easier it is to resist peer pressure.

METHOD: Classroom Activity

TIME FRAME: 5 minutes plus discussion time

MATERIALS NEEDED: None

ACTIVITY: Have each student choose a partner. Have them stand back to back with their partners. (This helps you to determine who has a partner and gets the activity organized faster.) Once everyone has a partner, have them all turn towards you so that you can teach them four hand motions. Show them the following hand motions and have them repeat them before you go on to the next one. In the first motion they are to put both hands on top of their head as if they were making rabbit ears. This hand motion is called the "rabbit". Next have them bring their hands down to their ears and put their thumbs in their ears with their palms facing forward. This hand motion is called the "moose". Next have them put both hands under their chin. Have them wiggle their fingers. This represents the hair on the chin of the "buffalo". Last, have them bring their hands down to their sides and flex them like they are a weight lifter. As they do this motion, they need to make a growling sound. This hand motion is called the "gorilla" (and yes I know that gorillas don't growl). Now repeat the hand motions with them following along so you can be sure they remember all four motions.

Once this is accomplished, have them once again stand back to back with their partner. Explain that you are going to count to three, and then they are to turn around and do one of those four hand motions to their partner. After they have done this, tell them that if they matched hand motions with their partner they may sit down. Have those that did not match go back to back with their partners again. Tell those that are sitting down to help you watch for matching pairs. After the second round, once again have those that match sit down. Do a third and final round for any of the pairs that are left. If they don't match on the third round, you can stop the activity.

DISCUSSION IDEAS:
* Why did you choose the hand motion that you did for the first round?
* Why did you choose the hand motion that you did for the second and third rounds?

- Since all of the hand motions were just made up without any real significance to any one of them, did it really matter which one you chose?
- How many of you on the first round chose the one that just felt right for you without a whole lot of other thoughts entering into your mind?
- What changes did you make when you needed to make a choice on the second or third round?
- What can this activity tell us about saying "no" when we are in a harmful or dangerous situation?
- List some of the different ways that you can say "no"?
- Would you use the same method in every situation? Why or why not?
- Describe some situations and tell how you would say "no".

GROUP SCULPTURE

TOPIC AREAS: Alcohol, Communication, Decision Making, Other Drugs

CONCEPT: Some of the things that seem so easy to us become very difficult when we are under the influence of drugs. This activity will start out very simple and then get harder. We will be able to see how being impaired slows down our ability to accomplish easy tasks. The exercise can also be used to demonstrate how important clear communication is when trying to accomplish a task in a group setting. The questions of leadership, decision making and understanding all come into play.

METHOD: Classroom Activity

TIME FRAME: 20 minutes plus discussion time

MATERIALS NEEDED:
- One blindfold for each person
- Two ropes that are long enough for half of the people in the group to hold on to at one time (about 30 feet for 15 people)

ACTIVITY: Divide the group into two teams with close to equal numbers on each team. Have the teams stand in a circle and throw a rope that is long enough for each team member to hang onto at one time in to the middle of the circle. Explain to the teams that you are going to call out a shape and they are going to see which team can pick up the rope and form that shape the fastest.

Pick shapes such as a square, triangle, circle, hexagon or pentagon. Between each shape have the rope thrown back into the middle of the circle.

Now have the groups put on their blindfolds and repeat the above activities. You will have to caution them against cheating by peeking out from under their blindfolds. You can repeat as many shapes as you would like, depending upon the amount of time you have to devote to the activity. One shape will be enough to get the discussion points across. The easiest shape for them to do blindfolded is a triangle. The more people involved, the harder the task. If you want more challenge, tie your ropes together for the blindfolded time and have the entire group try to form the shapes. You should not be the judge of when the group is finished with a shape. Have the group decide and tell you when they are satisfied with their shape before they remove their blindfolds.

DISCUSSION IDEAS:
- How hard was it for the group to create the shapes when they were not blindfolded?
- How did the group decide on how each shape was going to be created? Did leaders emerge? How were they chosen?
- Did you feel pressure by having another team to compete against?
- How was it different when you were blindfolded?
- Did the decision making process on how to form your shapes change when you were blindfolded? In what way?
- Did leadership become more or less important when you were blindfolded? Why do you think this was?
- Did everyone participate equally in the decision making process? Explain.

- What kinds of things made this task difficult to do when blindfolded?
- Did any of you become frustrated during this activity? Why?
- How did you handle your frustration?
- What can this activity teach us about working together?
- What can this activity teach us about group decision making?
- What can this activity teach us about solving problems or doing tasks when impaired by alcohol or other drugs?
- What can this activity teach us about communication?

GROUP TREASURE HUNT

TOPIC AREA: Self Esteem

CONCEPT: Each person is unique. This uniqueness is what makes our society work. If we were all the same, with similar interests, backgrounds, skills and characteristics, our society would be missing much of its creativity. This diversity allows for multiple points of view, with the end result being various perspectives to problems or situations. Telling students that they are unique seems to gloss over what actually makes them unique. By discussing various topics on how we are unique, we can get kids thinking about diversity and how valuable that is for society.

METHOD: Classroom Activity

TIME FRAME: 25 minutes plus discussion time

MATERIALS NEEDED:
- One pencil per team of five people
- One handout per team of five people

ACTIVITY: Divide your group into teams of five. Give each group a pencil and a scoring sheet. Have each team designate a recorder. This person will total the points for each question and keep a combined running total after each question is answered. Explain that scoring involves a team total which is the combined points for all members of the team. To keep all teams on the same question, you will read the questions one at a time, and go on when you feel all groups have finished.

You may wish to clarify the questions, depending on your age group. Allow for discussion time after each question since part of the intent of this activity is to allow an exchange among the team members about their answers. This permits the team to discover the uniqueness of the various team members. If time permits, you can have each team read out their scores after each question and keep track of which team has the most points by question. The purpose of this would be to point out during the discussion that the same team did not have the most points for all of the questions. After all of the questions have been answered, have the teams read out their total running scores. Don't play this up too much since the object of the activity is not to produce a winning team, but to provide a forum for interaction among team members.

TREASURE HUNT QUESTIONS

1. One point for each person living in your home.
2. One point for each button on your clothes.
3. One point for each team member who was born outside of the state.
4. One point for each pet in your family. (Fish only count as one pet)
5. One point for each team member with brown hair.
    Two points for each team member with blonde hair.
    Three points for each team member with black hair
    Four points for each team member with red hair.
    Five points for each team member with a hair color not listed above.
6. One point for each shoelace hole or hook on one shoe of each team member.
7. One point for each team member who has been in a state other than this one.

8. One point for each team member who has flown in an airplane.
9. One point for each musical instrument team members know how to play.
10. One point for each organized sports team that you have participated on in the past year.

DISCUSSION IDEAS:
- List ways in which people are different.
- Can all differences between people be seen when you look at someone? Why not?
- Are differences among people important? Why or why not?
- How do differences among people help our society?
- What would happen if everyone was the same?
- How did differences show themselves during the activity?
- Are some differences more important than others?
- Was everyone able to answer every question? Why not?
- Are any two or more people the same? Why not?
- How can people be similar but not the same?
- How important is it to have many types of people in a workplace?
- Why is it important to have people with various skills in a community?
- What characteristics among people in our society do we perceive as more desirable than others?
- How do society norms impact what we think about various individual differences or characteristics?

Score Sheet for Group Treasure Hunt

Total team points
for each question

Total combined team points
for all previously answered
questions

1. _____

2. _____

                                            Add points from question 1 & 2

3. _____

                                            Continue to add points together

4. _____

5. _____

6. _____

7. _____

8. _____

9. _____

10. _____

                                            This total is your combined
score for all ten questions

HOW BAD CAN YOU BE?

TOPIC AREA: Communication

CONCEPT: Your body language and other behavior play a major role in how successful your communication with others will be. This activity is presented through an "oppositional teaching" approach; it allows people to experience how others feel when they are not using "good listening skills". This is much more effective than just talking about what "good listening skills" are and how you should use them.

METHOD: Classroom Activity

TIME FRAME: 20 minutes plus discussion time

MATERIALS NEEDED:
- One felt tipped marker for each group of three to four people
- One large piece of paper for each group of three to four people
- One roll of masking tape

ACTIVITY: Break the class up into small groups of three or four. Give each group a large piece of paper and a magic marker. Have them spread themselves out around the room and make a list of what they would consider to be good listening skills. After about ten minutes, have them regroup and allow each group time to share their list with the entire class. Use masking tape to display the list in front of the room after each group has shared. When everyone has finished, go back and put a star on the papers next to the skills that were listed repeatedly.

Now have each person in the room choose a partner. Once they have all paired up, have them decide which person of the two is the tallest. The tallest person is the leader. Explain to them that now that they know what "good listening skills" are, they are going to experience "poor listening skills". The leader will tell about a vacation or trip that he took with his family. While he is telling the story, the other partner is to exhibit "poor listening skills". Let them do this for about a minute and then have them reverse roles so that both partners get to experience the entire activity.

DISCUSSION IDEAS:

- What were some of the things the person did who wasn't listening to you?
- How did you feel when you were the one telling the story?
- What kinds of words can we use to describe how you felt when you were telling the story?
- How did you feel when you were the one showing "poor listening skills"?
- What can this activity tell us about communication?
- Describe a situation that you have seen where this type of activity took place.
- What was the outcome of that situation?
- How did the participants feel?
- Was there good communication? Why not?
- How can we be sure that we are not a part of creating this kind of a problem?

HOW DOES IT FEEL?

TOPIC AREAS: Cliques, Values

CONCEPT: The usual reason for cliques is that one group feels superior to others. For this reason they exclude others from joining their group. This superiority may come from something they have in common such as good looks, athletics or money. Or this feeling may come from something about the other person that they feel makes that group or person inferior to them. Either way, the result is the same. A group or individual is excluded from participation. This exclusion may be done consciously or subconsciously, but the result is the same. It results in a lowering of self-esteem for those excluded and a false sense of self-esteem for those doing the excluding. One such group that is routinely dealt with in such a manner is the handicapped or physically disabled. This activity can fill two objectives. You can show how it feels to be different and at the same time develop some empathy in your students for those who are physically disabled.

METHOD: Classroom Demonstration

TIME FRAME: Half day to a full day

MATERIALS NEEDED:
- As many wheel chairs as you can borrow from the local hospital, doctor's office, Easter Seals office or medical supply store

ACTIVITY: Each person in your group is to spend a

half day or better yet a full day doing his normal rou-
tine in the confines of a wheel chair. This activity
makes even more impact if you can have them go into
an environment where people do not know they are only
in the wheel chair as an experiment. Since you probably
won't be able to have your entire class in wheel chairs
on the same day, have them write down how they felt
during the day so they can refer back to these notes
when you have your discussion.

VARIATION:
This activity can also be done with crutches.

DISCUSSION IDEAS:
• What was different about being in a wheel chair?
• What things were more difficult for you to do?
• How did people treat you differently when you were
  in a wheel chair?
• How did you feel when you were in the wheel chair?
• How did you feel when people who didn't know you
  looked at you?
• List some of the emotions you felt while in the
  wheel chair.
• Was there ever a time during the day that you
  wished you could get up and behave non-handi-
  capped?
• How do you think people who are confined to wheel
  chairs for the rest of their lives feel?
• Handicapped people are just one group at our
  school. What are some of the other groups?
• How well do all of the groups get along with each
  other?
• Do most people hang around with the same group
  most of the time? Why or why not?
• Do certain groups feel better than other groups?
  Why or why not?

- How hard is it to join a new group? Explain.
- What do you have to do to fit in?
- What happens if you don't fit in? How does this make you feel?
- Describe a situation where you or a friend had trouble fitting into a group.
- How can we help people fit into groups that we belong to?
- How can we make others feel comfortable around a new group?
- What can we do when we want to fit into a new group?
- Handicapped people have a disability that we can see. What are some disabilities that we can't see?
- Are these any less of a disability?
- How should we act around those with a disability?
- Are disabled people any different emotionally from those without a disability? Why or why not?

I'LL BET YOU CAN'T

TOPIC AREAS: Goal Setting, Peer Pressure

CONCEPT: Others have a great impact on our behavior. Those who we know best have the greatest impact. This activity gives the participants a chance to ignore those trying to get them to negatively change their behavior. As they play the game, they will find out that those who they know best are the ones who have the easiest time making them do what they don't want to do.

METHOD: Classroom activity

TIME FRAME: 15 minutes plus discussion time

MATERIALS NEEDED: None

ACTIVITY: Have the class line up in two lines facing each other. The first two people in each line will walk side-by-side down between the lines. They must keep their eyes up and walk at a normal pace down the aisle. Their goal is to reach the end of the line without cracking a smile. If one of the two walkers smile before they reach the end of the line, then they join the opposing team's line. If both walkers smile while passing through the gauntlet, then they each join the lines of the opposing team. The job of those standing in the lines is to get the walkers to smile. They may do anything they want except to touch or harm the walkers in any way. You can have the walkers pass next to their own team or the opposing team. The game is over when everyone has had a turn at passing through the walk. The team with the most players in their line at the end of the game is declared the winner.

DISCUSSION IDEAS:

- Did anyone find it hard not to smile as they walked down the line? Why?
- What kinds of behavior did others use to make you smile?
- What kinds of behaviors were the most effective on you?
- Were these behaviors the same for everyone? Why not?
- Were there certain people that were better at making you smile than others? Why were some able to make you smile and you could ignore others?
- How did you feel when you were one of the people trying to make them smile?
- Was it easy to make people smile even when they didn't want to? Why?
- How can we apply this activity to peer pressure?
- How can this activity apply to goal setting?
- How much concentration did it take to keep from smiling?
- Why is it easier to accomplish something when you concentrate on it?
- What role does your behavior play in accomplishing your goals?
- Which is more important, the way you think about reaching a goal or the way you act when trying to reach a goal? Why?
- What role do other people play in you reaching your goals?
- How can other people help you reach your goals?
- How can other people hinder you in trying to reach your goals?
- What could the people in this activity have done to help you reach the end of the line without smiling?

IN THE DRIVER'S SEAT

TOPIC AREAS: Addiction, Alcohol, Other Drugs

CONCEPT: The use of certain drugs cause physiological changes in your body. These chemicals inhibit your thinking processes and your physical reactions. To some degree or another, you are giving up control over your actions to the drug. The amount of use, frequency of use and choice of drug will determine how much control you are giving up. At some point, addiction becomes a problem and you become totally under the control of the drug. Most people want to be in control of what happens to them. We need to address that the use of alcohol and other drugs takes some of that control away from the individual and gives it to the chemical. People take risks, say things, do things and are involved in situations such as sexual activity and lawlessness, that they would not otherwise be a part of if they were in total control of their thoughts and actions.

METHOD: Classroom Activities

TIME FRAME: 15 minutes plus discussion time

MATERIALS NEEDED:
- One blindfold for every two people
- One to three baseball hats or some other item that can be used to distinguish who is "it".

ACTIVITY: The activity is basically a game of tag. Establish boundaries for the game. The area should not be too big. You don't want the game to involve too much running. Have everyone get a partner. One person from each pair will need to get a blindfold and put it on. The "sighted" person will stand behind the blindfolded person with their hands on the blindfolded person's shoulders. The game of tag is played in pairs. You will designate a team as being "it". Give them the baseball hat to wear so everyone will know they are "it". The rules are that only the blindfolded person from the team that is "it", may tag another team. The person they tag must be the blindfolded person from another pair. If they tag the "sighted" person, then it doesn't count. When a tag is made, the baseball hat is transferred to the team that is now "it". Have the partners switch places during the game so that they will experience both positions: blind and sighted.

VARIATION: If you would like to make the game even more challenging, assign more than one team to be "it" at a time.

A word here about safety: Emphasize that caution must be taken during the game. You can imagine what will take place during this activity. The person who can see will be moving his partner all over the area. The person who is blindfolded will be at the mercy of the "sighted" partner to keep him from being tagged. Unsportsmanlike conduct will cause a team to be disqualified and removed from the activity.

DISCUSSION IDEAS:
* What did you see taking place during this activity?
* Was being the person who could see easier or was it easier to be the person who was blindfolded? Why?
* Which position did you like the best?
* How much control did the person without the blindfold have?

- How much control did the person with the blindfold have?
- How did it feel to be out of control when you were blindfolded?
- How can we relate this activity to the control that alcohol and other drugs have over our lives?
- Once your brain is affected by a drug, how much control do you have over your actions?
- Should a person who is out of control because of drugs be excused for his actions since he didn't know what he was doing? Why?
- Describe some situations you would not want to be in when you were under the influence.
- List some occupations where being under the influence would endanger the safety of others.
- Would you get in the car with a person who was drunk? Why or why not?
- How would you get out of a situation where you needed a ride home but the person who was supposed to give you one was under the influence?
- How can this activity relate to addiction?
- Are people who are addicted controlling their own lives? Why or why not?
- How can using drugs interfere with the goals and dreams that you have for your life?

JOGGING IN PLACE

TOPIC AREA: Tobacco

CONCEPT: When a person smokes a cigarette he is inhaling tar into his lungs. The lungs have tiny sacs called "alveoli". These sacs allow the breathing process to work. Some of the tar that makes its way into the lungs becomes deposited in these tiny air sacs. Two things can occur. First, the sacs can become filled up with tar and cease to function. Second, the air sacs can fill up with tar and burst. Either way it reduces the ability of your lungs to do their job. When this occurs, you experience a shortness of breath. When it becomes severe it is called emphysema. But you don't have to have the disease emphysema to have reduced breathing capacity. This can occur a short time after you begin smoking. Here is a bit of trivia for you: the tar that comes from cigarettes is the same tar that is used to make asphalt roads. If you were to smoke one pack of cigarettes per day for a year, you would be inhaling the equivalent of a quart jar of tar into your lungs per year.

METHOD: Classroom Activity

TIME FRAME: 5 minutes plus discussion time

MATERIALS NEEDED:
• One drinking straw for each of your students

ACTIVITY: Have your students stand up. Tell them to jog in place. Pretend that you are running up hill, down hill and across a flat field. Remind them to take good strong deep breaths as they do this. Now stop them and pass out a straw to each student. Repeat the same process, but this time remind them that they can only breath through the straw. Do not allow this part of the activity to go on so long that students feel faint. Collect the straws before going on to the processing stage.

DISCUSSION IDEAS:
- How did you feel when you were jogging the first time?
- How did you feel when you were jogging and breathing through the straw?
- How many of you had trouble running hard and breathing through the straw?
- Did any of you feel light headed when breathing through the straw?
- How do you think this activity relates to smoking?
- What can this activity tell us about smoking?
- What activities can you think of that would be hard to do if you were a smoker?
- What kinds of activities would you like to do in the future that would be more difficult if you were a smoker?

LEFT OUT

TOPIC AREA: Cliques

CONCEPT: There are very few situations in a young person's life that are more traumatic than being left out of the "in group", whatever that is at the moment. The wanting to belong is so strong that we see kids getting mixed up with groups that they may not really want to be a part of, but they are desperate to be a part of something. This may be where some of the interest in gangs has come from in recent years. This activity addresses the problem from the person's point of view who is on the outside looking in.

METHOD: Classroom Activity

TIME FRAME: 10 minutes plus discussion

MATERIALS NEEDED: None

ACTIVITY: Have the entire class stand up and gather in a circle. Explain that the object of this activity will be to follow the commands you give. You will call out a number and they will have to form themselves into groups that are made up of that number. Between each command, be sure that the group mills around. If they don't, then the same people will always group together. For the first few times let them practice and see how fast they can do it. If there are any people left over after the groups have been formed, they are to just stand still and jump back in the game during the next command.

As an example, you will call out the number three. Everyone in the group has to find two partners and form a group of three people. Give them only about three to five seconds to find a group. Before you call out another number, be sure that the group mills around. Then you might call out five, no one may stay in the same group so everyone goes looking for a new group of five people. After a few practice rounds, explain that from now on if you do not get in a group then you must go to the side and stand. These people are out of the game. The game continues until you have only a few people left and you call out the number two. Someone loses and the couples that are left are the winners. I would recommend that you play this elimination round through at least twice before you stop.

DISCUSSION IDEAS:
- Was there anything hard about this activity? What was it?
- How did you feel when you were not able to join a group and were out of the game?
- What words can we use to describe these feelings?
- How easy was it to keep finding a new group to join every time a new number was called out?
- What is a clique?
- What can this activity teach us about cliques?
- Are cliques bad or good? Explain
- Describe the different groups that are found in your school.
- How do some people feel when they are not in a group?
- Does everyone want to be a part of a group? Explain
- What are the advantages of being in a group?
- Are certain groups such as Cheerleaders, Jocks, Nerds, etc. stereotyped as to how they act?
- What are the stereotypes and are they true?

LIGHTS - CAMERA - ACTION

TOPIC AREA: Advertising

CONCEPT: The advertising media portrays the use of alcohol and tobacco in a very positive light. Through the use of young models, upbeat situations, cartoon characters, expensive ads and contemporary music, their appeal is definitely to the young. All prevention programs need to expose advertising for what it really is. Kids need to be able to analyze for themselves what the message of the ads are and how they slant the truth to be most beneficial to their product. This is true of all advertising, not just alcohol and drug advertising. This activity calls for a careful look at today's ads and then counters with some advertising that looks at the other side of the picture.

METHOD: Classroom Activity

TIME FRAME: 45 minutes plus discussion time

MATERIALS NEEDED:
- Examples of advertising, both TV and magazine
- Construction paper, scissors, felt tipped markers if print ads are to be done
- Video camera and TV if filming is to be done

ACTIVITY: You need to bring examples of advertising to class. You can tape some television commercials and bring them in to show. You can have the kids in your class bring in ads from magazines that they would like to analyze. After the class has looked at some of the advertising that has been brought in, divide the class into groups of three or four. Have them choose an ad idea that they would like to plan a counter ad about. The idea is for them to see what the ad is saying and counter that with another statement that might be more truthful than the ad itself.

The counter ads could be done with construction paper, felt tipped markers and pictures from magazines. These would then be explained in front of the class and later displayed in the school halls. You could have the students do a TV commercial that is a spoof on the current popular TV commercials for beer products. If you have them plan a TV commercial, they should perform it in front of the class or video tape it and show it at a Parent's Night or in another classroom at your school.

DISCUSSION IDEAS:
- How truthful are the ads that we looked at from television and magazines?
- What is the meaning of a "half-truth"?
- If the ads were really truthful do you think people would buy the product?
- What techniques do advertisers use to make their product appealing?
- Do the ads look like they are targeted to older people or younger people?
- Why would the companies want to target younger people?
- What techniques do advertisers use to attract the younger audience?
- What can this activity teach us about advertising?
- Do you think we should ban all advertising of alcohol and tobacco products?

- Do you think the people who create this kind of advertising are bad or immoral people?
- Is advertising made up of mostly lies? Explain.
- What is the purpose of advertising?
- Does advertising fulfill its purpose?
- Have you ever bought something or gone to see a movie because of advertising? Describe the situation.

LINE UP

TOPIC AREA: Self Esteem

CONCEPT: One of the ideas we try to stress in the area of self esteem is the concept of each person's uniqueness. This activity will show that everyone in the class has something to contribute that is unique to that person.

METHOD: Classroom Activity

TIME FRAME: 10 to 15 minutes

MATERIALS NEEDED: None

ACTIVITY: Divide the class into groups of about twelve to fifteen people. Have them line up in single file lines, by group, facing you. The object of the activity is for them to line up according to whatever category that you call out. When they feel they have lined up correctly, every member of the team must raise their hand or sit down wherever they are in line. As an example, you might say "Please line up by height, shortest in front and tallest in the back, Go!". Each team would rearrange themselves as quickly as they could in a single file line with the shortest person in the front and the tallest person in the back. The first to team accomplish the task and give the appropriate finish signal would be declared the winner and another task will be called out.

Some additional suggested line up categories:
By shoe size
By hair color
By hair length
By width of your smile
By eye color
By number of kids in the family
By birthday
By number of pets your family owns at the moment
By the number of visible buttons on your clothes
Etc.

DISCUSSION IDEAS:
- What did you see happening in this activity?
- Did people stay the same place during each of the commands? Why not?
- Which people are the most important ones in this activity, the ones in the front or the ones in the back? Why?
- Were you always between the same people? Why not?
- What can this activity tell us about people being different?
- Is it good or bad to be different than each other?
- How would the world be different if we were all the same?
- Let's list on the board some of the things that make us unique.
- How does this uniqueness show itself in our lives as we grow older?

LIVER OVERLOAD

TOPIC AREA: Alcohol

CONCEPT: This activity is an attempt to show how the liver becomes overloaded when too much alcohol is introduced into the bloodstream. The liver is able to detoxify approximately one can of beer, one glass of wine or one and a half ounces of alcohol per hour. If alcohol is introduced into the bloodstream any faster than this, then the liver can not do its job fast enough. When this happens, the alcohol is left in the bloodstream and the BAC (Blood Alcohol Content) count rises. This simply means that the percentage of alcohol in the blood is getting higher.

METHOD: Classroom Demonstration

TIME FRAME: 10 minutes plus discussion time

MATERIALS NEEDED:
* Fifteen tennis balls

ACTIVITY: Bring five students up in front of the class. Have them stand in a single file line, shoulder to shoulder facing the class. Designate one person at one end of the line as the "Liver". You will stand at the end of the line away from the "Liver". You will hand a tennis ball to the first person in line. He will pass the ball down the line until it reaches the "Liver". The person who is representing the "Liver" will have to squeeze the tennis ball ten times before he can drop the ball to the floor. This action represents the detoxification of the alcohol from the blood. Start by sending the tennis balls down the line slowly. Each person may only be holding one tennis ball at a time. At this speed the "Liver" will not have too tough a time getting in his ten squeezes before he receives the next tennis ball that is passed down the line. This will give the class a chance to see how the body's liver is supposed to function.

Now regather all of the tennis balls. This time send them down the line faster. They will find that the "Liver" is not able to detoxify the blood fast enough to keep up with the rate that you are introducing new tennis balls into the line or "bloodstream". Pretty soon there will be people just holding the tennis balls in their hands waiting for the "Liver" to get done with its ten squeezes so the next ball can be sent to it. This back log of tennis balls in the bloodstream will represent the alcohol that is waiting to be detoxified. This is a graphic example of how a high BAC in the body is reached.

DISCUSSION IDEAS:
- What did you see happening when the tennis balls were being introduced slowly into the bloodstream?
- What did you see happening when the tennis balls were being introduced more quickly into the bloodstream?
- What do you think would happen to a liver who experienced this very often?
- What happens to the body when the alcohol is not detoxified by the liver?
- What do you think this activity can tell us about alcohol and our bodies?
- If it is the liver that detoxifies our body from alcohol, what does that say about having a person who is drunk, drink coffee or take a cold shower to try and sober up?

MAGIC CUP

TOPIC AREA: Peer Pressure

CONCEPT: Peer pressure usually works best on those that are least prepared to handle it. If you have made a decision not to use drugs then you are more likely to refuse any attempts to get you to "see what it is like". This protection can be provided by knowledge about the harmful effects of drugs. It can also be provided by practicing or role playing ways to say "no" before the situation arises. It can also be your friends who help you stand up to those who feel that using is the cool thing to do. You are going to heat up water in a paper cup. The water will get hot and the paper cup that is not protected by water will burn up, but the paper cup that is protected by water will be unharmed.

METHOD: Classroom Demonstration

TIME FRAME: 10 minutes plus discussion time

MATERIALS NEEDED:
- At least two paper cups (the ones with a light wax coating work the best)
- Some kind of heat source with a flame, such as a camping stove
- Water and matches

ACTIVITY: Light the stove and after the flames get going real good, place one of the paper cups on the stove and watch it catch on fire. Now place a cup that is half full of water on the stove. The portion of the cup that does not have water in it might catch on fire. If it does, go ahead and let it burn. But have the class notice that the paper cup that is protected by the water is not catching on fire. Let the experiment go on long enough that the water becomes hot. You may let it go long enough that the water starts to boil.

DISCUSSION IDEAS:

- What did you see happening to the first cup?
- What did you see happening to the second cup?
- Why did only part of the cup with water in it burn?
- What protected the rest of the cup from burning?
- How can we relate this experiment to resisting peer pressure?
- What are some of the ways that you can use to help you say no when someone asks you to do something you know is wrong?
- What are some of the situations that you can get into which would require you to use some of these techniques?
- Describe a situation where you have had to say no when someone asked you to join them in doing something you knew was wrong.
- How easy is it to say no to a stranger that is pressuring you to do something harmful? Why?
- How easy is it to say no to your friends when they ask you to join them in a harmful activity? Why?
- What does this suggest about the kinds of friends that you should have?
- If your friends are always pressuring you to join them in questionable activities, what should you do?

MARSHMALLOW TOWER

TOPIC AREAS: Decision Making, Problem Solving

CONCEPT: Sometimes the decisions we make are not ours alone to make. There might be a group of people involved. You need to know how decisions are made in a group and the dynamics that take place. Our ability to influence a group decision will play a major role in our staying out of trouble since many of our troubles occur in groups and not by ourselves.

METHOD: Classroom Activity

TIME FRAME: 20 minutes plus discussion time

MATERIALS NEEDED:
- Approximately 75 round toothpicks and 100 miniature marshmallows for every six people.
- A watch with a second hand on it.

ACTIVITY: Divide your group into smaller groups of six people each. Give each group a handful of toothpicks and a pile of miniature marshmallows. They may get more toothpicks or marshmallows from you if they run out. Explain that the object of the activity is to have each small group build the tallest, free standing tower that they can. They will have ten minutes to complete the building of their tower. In exactly ten minutes, you will call time and every team must take their hands off of their tower. Exactly fifteen seconds later you will judge the towers to see which one is the tallest. This means that the tower must still be standing, without any help from the group or any other devices for fifteen seconds.

DISCUSSION IDEAS:
- How did you decide what the tower was going to look like?
- Did you come up with a plan before you started or did you just start and make changes as you went? Was this a good or bad method? Why?
- Was a leader chosen in your group? Did one emerge? How was your group led?
- Was your end product satisfactory? What would you change next time?
- What can this activity tell us about making decisions?
- Describe the roles that each person in your group played.
- Were some people in your group more involved than others? Why?

MIND POWER

TOPIC AREA: Goal Setting

CONCEPT: We have more power in our minds than we ever use. Some researchers feel that we use only about ten percent of our brain power. There is a term called self-fulfilling prophecy which means that what we think is what will take place. We seem to be magnetically drawn towards the things that we think about. This theory has been formalized in what some people refer to as "self talk": What we say to ourselves becomes what we believe. Of course you don't want to take this too far - just because we think about food all the time doesn't mean we will turn into a hamburger. But researchers have shown that in many cases what our minds dwell upon is the direction our lives move. When we set a goal, we concentrate on achieving that goal and take actions that will bring it to pass. Many times the actions and decisions we make are not even made consciously, but they turn out helping us accomplish our goal even without the conscious thought.

METHOD: Classroom Activity

TIME FRAME: 10 minutes plus discussion time

MATERIALS NEEDED:
- You will need one quarter inch flat metal washer and a fifteen inch string for each person in your class. Tie one end of the string through the hole in the washer.

ACTIVITY: Have each student hold their string up in front of their face so that the washer hangs about six inches away from their eyes. This position will make it look like they are going to try and hypnotize themselves. Their arms, elbows and hands must not be touching anything such as a desk or a chair. Now have them stop the washer from swinging by using their other hand to stop it's motion. Tell them that they are going to make the washer start to swing by just using their eyes. Have them focus their eyes on the washer and slowly start to move their eyes back and forth while holding their hand still. While they are doing this you should be slowly saying "left to right, left to right, left to right". Repeat this phrase over and over again until their washers start to swing back and forth.

If you want to really amaze them, change the commands to "front to back, front to back, front to back". Tell them to move their eyes up and down while watching the washer. The washer will slowly change directions and start moving front to back. Now change the command to "around and around". Have them move their eyes in a circle and watch the washer. It will slowly start moving in a circle. For the advanced kids, you can have them move their eyes in a circle the opposite way and the washer will stop it's circle and start going the opposite way.

This is not magic. About ninety percent of your kids will be able to control the washer to some degree. Much of it depends on their concentration and how little distractions they receive from others in the group. The reason that this exercise works is the mind sends messages to the hand to move the washer in the same direction as the commands you are saying. Those individuals with "fine motor skills" will be able to have it respond best. Those with less well developed fine motor skills or little concentration will see little or no movement.

DISCUSSION IDEAS:

- How many of you were able to make the washer follow my commands?
- How many of you found it easy to make it do what you wanted it to do?
- What were some of the factors that made this activity difficult for some to accomplish?
- How do you think this exercise can relate to goal setting?
- How many of you talk to yourself?
- What are the kinds of things that you say to yourself?
- Do you feel that your actions are influenced by what you think and say to yourself? Why or why not?
- In what kinds of activities do you feel that thoughts or self talk would have an impact on your behavior?
- How do we feel about what others say about us?
- How does what others say about us influence our behavior?
- How can we overcome what others are saying about us?
- Which is more important, what others say about us or what we say about ourselves? Why?

MOUNT EVEREST

TOPIC AREAS: Decision Making, Problem Solving

CONCEPT: Students need to learn how to influence others in a group setting and make a group decision. This activity gives the group a problem and asks them to solve it. To do so, the members must converse among themselves and decide upon the best method of solution. The dynamics of leadership and influencing group opinion are both in play. Many decisions to participate in harmful behavior are made in groups rather than as individuals. If we do not equip our students with the skills needed to help form group opinion, then we doom them to the fate of being a follower even when the decision is a poor one.

METHOD: Classroom Activity

TIME FRAME: 20 minutes plus discussion time

MATERIALS NEEDED:
- A piece of masking tape for each team
- A wall that is approximately eighteen feet high. (The inside of a gym or the side of a building are good places to check.)

ACTIVITY: Form teams of five people. Be sure that each team has the same number of large and small sized people on it. The team's assignment is to place one piece of masking tape as high as they can on the wall using nothing to help them but the other members of the team. If possible, have most of the teams attempt the activity at the same time. By doing this, they can't spend a lot of time studying what methods the other teams are using to place their masking tape. If there is not enough room, simply have the waiting teams situated so they can not watch what is going on too closely. Use individuals from other teams to be spotters, to help in case someone falls. They should be placed behind the team and be ready to help.

Caution! This can be a dangerous activity if strict guidelines are not followed. No one may be thrown or may jump at any time during the activity. Each team must have a minimum of two spotters standing behind them if they attempt to put people on their shoulders, or if they attempt any other method that involves leaving the ground. The teacher is the final word on what techniques may be dangerous.

DISCUSSION IDEAS:
- Describe the different techniques that were used.
- Which techniques worked the best? Why?
- Which techniques did not prove to be effective? Why?
- Did your group have a leader? If so how was that person chosen?
- How were decisions made in the group to decide what should be tried?
- Was everyone on the team equally involved in the decision making process? If not, please explain why. If yes, please describe how this worked.
- How could more people have been involved in the decision making process?
- Have you ever been in a situation where a decision was made for you by someone else in a group? Describe the situation.

- How does it make you feel when others make decisions that effect you?
- How can you best influence a group decision?
- If no one is listening, what behavior can you use to be heard?
- Which of the behaviors listed above are the most effective? Why?
- Which of the behaviors listed above are the least effective? Why?
- What should you do if the group makes a decision that involves you, but you feel may be harmful to your health, dangerous or illegal?

PASS RIGHT - PASS LEFT

TOPIC AREA: Communication

CONCEPT: Certain skills for good communication are certainly more important than others. One of the most important of these is the skill of listening. This activity will show the importance of listening and how difficult that is when you are not concentrating on what is being said because your busy doing something else.

METHOD: Classroom Activity

TIME FRAME: 10 minutes plus discussion time

MATERIALS NEEDED:
- The Wright Family Story
- One button or some other small item for each person in the group

ACTIVITY: Have your entire group form a circle. The best format is to have them seated on the floor sitting "Indian" style. If this will not work with your group, you can have them in chairs or even standing in a circle. Give each person in the circle a penny or some other small item that can be passed easily from hand to hand. Tell the group that you are going to read them a story and every time they hear any word that sounds like right or left, they are to pass the button in their hand to the person on their right or left depending on what they heard. Start reading the story slowly so that they have a chance to catch on to what you want them to do. After a few passes stop the story and ask them how they are doing. Check to see that everyone has a button in his hand. If your group is typical, some will have two or three buttons and others will not have any. Have them redistribute the buttons so that everyone has one again. Now continue to read the story, getting faster as you go. Stop the story a couple of more times to check on how they are doing.

DISCUSSION IDEAS:
- What was happening during this activity?
- What made the activity difficult to accomplish?
- What impact did what other people do have on your ability to stay up with the story?
- How did you feel during the activity?
- What would have made the activity easier to accomplish?
- How hard was it to listen and pass the objects at the same time?
- How much of the story can you remember?
- How seriously did everyone take the activity?
- What impact did the level of seriousness have on the activity?
- What can this activity tell us about communication?
- How hard were you concentrating during the activity?
- How hard were the people concentrating on either side of you?
- How does this level of concentration compare with what you do when someone is talking to you?
- Describe a situation you have had where someone was not really listening to you when you were telling them something?
- How did that make you feel?

LIFE WITH THE WRIGHT FAMILY

One day the Wright family decided to take a vacation. The first thing they had to decide was who would be left at home since there was not enough room in the Wright family car for all of them. Mr. Wright decided that Aunt Linda Wright would be the one left at home. Of course this made Aunt Linda Wright so mad that she left the house immediately yelling "It will be a right cold day before I return".

The Wright family now bundled up the children, Tommy Wright, Susan Wright, Timmy Wright and Shelly Wright and got in the car and left. Unfortunately, as they turned out of the driveway someone had left a trash can in the street so they had to turn right around and stop the car. They told Tommy Wright to get out of the car and move the trash can so they could get going. Tommy took so long that they almost left him in the street. Once the Wright family got on the road, Mother Wright wondered if she had left the stove on. Father Wright told her not to worry he had checked the stove and she had not left it on. As they turned right at the corner, everyone started to think about other things that they might have left undone.

No need to worry now, they were off on a right fine vacation. When they arrived at the gas station, Father Wright put gas in the car and then discovered that he had left his wallet at home. So Timmy Wright ran home to get the money that was left behind. After Timmy had left, Susan Wright started to feel sick. She left the car saying that she had to throw up. This of course got Mother Wright's attention and she left the car in a hurry. Shelly Wright wanted to watch Susan get sick, so she left the car too. Father Wright was left with Tommy Wright who was playing a game in the backseat.

With all of this going on Father Wright decided that this was not the right time to take a vacation, so he gathered up all of the family and left the gas station as quickly as he could. When he arrived home, he turned left into the driveway and said "I wish the Wright family had never left the house today!"

PEOPLE JUMP

TOPIC AREAS: Decision Making, Problem Solving

CONCEPT: In life there are many problems to solve. Sometimes these problems involve more than one person. We have to be able to think not only of ourselves, but of others. Actions that we take may have consequences that reach beyond ourselves. As we look at solutions to problems, we need to take all of the consequences into account not just the immediate ones. Many times the first solution to a problem is not the best one for ourselves or others. We need to keep our thoughts open to the alternatives that are available and to listen to the input of others. Once we have looked at all the available options, our decision can be made. We also need to learn how to make suggestions to a large group so that our input is not ignored.

METHOD: Classroom Activity

TIME FRAME: 20 minutes plus discussion time

MATERIALS NEEDED:
- A long thick rope that can be used as a jump rope. The rope must be long enough to fit as many people from your class jumping at one time in it as possible.

ACTIVITY: There are really two activities to this lesson. You may choose to do either or both. The objective of the first activity is to get each person in your class to go through the jump rope one at a time, make one jump while it is turning and run out the other side. If anyone messes up, then everyone that has gone through must start over again. If the class finds this easy to do, then have them do it again while racing against the clock to beat their own best time. The problem for the group (no help from you) will be to figure out what is the best order for the people to pass through the rope. After a couple of tries they will see that the best jumpers should not be the first ones through because they just have to go back when a less talented jumper doesn't make it. This is also a good time to talk about cheering and supporting others. If only your best jumpers continue to go through first, make a rule that each time everyone has to go back those people go to the end of the line.

The objective of the second activity is to see how many people you can get in the rope at one time and have all of them jump at least one revolution of the rope at the same time. The group will have to figure out a strategy for getting the most people jumping at one time. Anytime the rope is stopped, all the jumpers must exit. After a period of time if you see only the same few trying to get in, make the jumpers who are in when the rope is stopped be the last ones in the next time the group tries.

VARIATIONS: Have the group go through the turning rope and jump by twos, threes or fours.

It is very interesting in both of these activities to see who the leaders are, how suggestions are given and taken and what kind of support the group gives each other. If you feel some individuals are taking over, you can silence them for the rest of the activity or appoint leaders that are the only ones that can address the group. Everyone must bring their suggestions to these leaders and whisper them in their ear. This is of course a great way to see how some of your quieter kids react to the position of leader when given a chance.

DISCUSSION IDEAS:
- What problems did you have in the activities?
- What was easy about the activities?
- How were leaders chosen in the group?
- How were decisions made as to what strategies you would try?
- Were these methods of decision making effective?
- What could have been done to make the decision making process more effective?
- How often did you stop the activity and take time to think and talk about alternatives you could try?
- Was everyone just worried about getting themselves through the activity?
- How did you show that you were concerned with how successful others were in completing the activity?
- Did anyone feel frustrated during the activity? Explain.
- Was everyone involved in the decision making process? Explain.
- How did you feel about how the decisions were made?
- What can we learn about making decisions from this activity?
- What can we learn about working together from this activity?
- Describe some situations where a decision you make can impact others.

PEOPLE LIFT

TOPIC AREA: Goal Setting

CONCEPT: This activity shows that people can do more than they think they can when they focus their energy.

METHOD: Classroom Demonstration

TIME FRAME: 10 minutes plus discussion time

MATERIALS NEEDED:
* One straight backed chair

ACTIVITY: Have one student sit in the chair with his arms crossed and held out slightly away from his chest. Select four other students and have them stand two on each side of the seated student. Have two of these students stand beside each of the shoulders of the seated student and have the other two students stand beside each of the knees of the seated student. Have the standing students interlock their own two hands together with their two index fingers pointing out in front of them. Now have them, on the count of three, put their index fingers under the right arm and the other person under the left arm just forward of the arm pit area and just behind the bend of the right knee and of the left knee of the seated student and lift as hard as they can. They will not be able to lift the student very high off of the chair, if at all. For safety's sake, you should have someone standing directly behind the seated student to be sure that if he is lifted off the seat that he does not tip backwards. If the student is easily lifted off of the chair during this part of the activity, I would suggest that you choose a heavier student.

After you have gone through the activity described above, it is time to focus the student's energy. Bring the four students together and have them put their hands over the head of the seated student. As they are standing there, talk to them about how they need to focus their energy. To help them focus their energy have them join you in an exercise. Have them interlock their hands again and put them down in front of them. Tell them you are going to count to four. On the first three counts, have them take a deep breath and raise their hands above their head in a lifting motion, letting their breath out as they raise their hands. You will do this exercise with them, and ask the seated person to deep breath along with them. Then on the fourth count they are to stick their fingers back under the seated person and lift with all of their might. Once again be sure that you have a person behind the chair to protect against falling over. If the procedure has been done correctly, the group will be able to lift the person off of the chair quite easily. You must emphasize two factors: As you are going through the pep talk with the lifters, the breathing and the lifting simulation, both the class and the four students must be quiet and serious; laughter will distract the lifters and make the activity not work.

DISCUSSION IDEAS:
•   Ask the lifters how they felt when you first told them that they were going to lift the student by just using their two index fingers.
•   Ask the person in the chair how he felt in the same situation.

- Ask the class what their reaction was when you first explained the activity.
- Ask all concerned what they thought when you went through the practice exercises with them.
- Ask how the lifters and student felt when they were able to lift him off of the chair.
- What made the students able to lift the person the second time and not the first time?
- What would have happened if the lifters continued to laugh instead of taking the activity seriously?
- Why did the class have to be quiet during the second part of the activity?
- How does this activity relate to goal setting?
- Describe a situation where you or someone you know were able to accomplish something that at first seemed impossible.
- What are examples of goals people your age would set?

PORTHOLE

TOPIC AREAS: Decision Making, Problem Solving

CONCEPT: Getting a group to decide on a course of action is never easy. Just remember the last time you got together with a bunch of friends and tried to choose a place to go out to eat or which video to rent for the evening. With youth it is equally as tough if not tougher. They have not mastered the intricacies of making personal decisions, much less how to influence a group's decision. This is unfortunate since many of the problems that face our youth occur in a group setting. It is rare to find a kid out by himself drinking, drugging, vandalizing or shoplifting. This learning activity will give insight into how a group decision is reached and can allow your students practice this all important skill in a safe environment.

METHOD: Classroom Activity

TIME FRAME: 20 to 30 minutes plus discussion time

MATERIALS NEEDED:
- Something that forms a hoop, such as a small hula hoop, a bicycle inner tube or heavy wire that you have formed into a circle and is rather lightweight. The size should be about one foot greater in diameter than your widest student.
- A piece of lightweight rope or string
- A couple of chairs or desks

*It is best if the girls wear pants during this activity

ACTIVITY: If you have ever played Spider Web, this is a version of that but takes a shorter amount of time. Suspend the circle from the ceiling using your rope or string. It should hang with the lowest part of the circle at about belt height for the average student in your class. Place the two chairs at either side and in line with the hoop. Attach a rope or string to both sides of the hoop and tie them to the two chairs. This will suspend the circle in space and give it some rigidity. It doesn't have to be strong, but it does need to stay relatively stationary.

The activity starts with the entire group standing on one side of the hoop. (With younger groups you may want to allow one person to stand on the opposite side of the hoop to help the first person through. They would then return to the other side of the hoop to be passed through along with the rest of the group.) The object is to have everyone passed through the hoop with help from the group without anyone touching the hoop or supporting ropes. No part of anyone's body, except the person being passed through, may go past an imaginary line that extends in all directions from the hoop. This means that the person who is being passed through the hoop and those doing the passing must be very careful. If anyone touches the hoop, supporting ropes or extends any part of their body past the hoop, everyone must go back and start all over again. Even the person being passed through may not touch the hoop or supporting ropes. If you want to make this activity really hard, do not allow any talking. You could also allow them to plan for three minutes before they start and then require silence. I would not try these options the first time you attempt this activity.

Part of the learning process will be the frustration

they will have to endure when they have to start over again. I have had groups that have had to start over again a dozen times. The teacher's role is to judge when someone has touched the hoop sufficiently to send the entire group back. When the group reaches the last person, they may choose one person from the completed side to return and help this last person through the hoop. This is the only time someone may return to help. Once they are through the hoop, they must remain on the completed side unless the entire group is sent back.

You can see that there will be numerous false starts and plans that fail in this activity. Decisions will be made and leaders emerge that will cause frustration on the part of the group. Watch carefully so that you can help process who the leaders were and how they emerged. Watch to see if all ideas were listened to or just those from certain people. If the group becomes stuck on a certain plan and keeps trying it even though it is unsuccessful, stop them and ask questions. Get them to rethink their strategy and put their heads together. Do not give in and solve the problem for them.

Emphasize safety in this activity. Everyone needs to help each other to be sure that only safe moves are attempted. You should step in and stop any move that you can see will result in an unsafe lift or landing. If at all possible, this activity should be done with twelve to fifteen participants. If your class is larger, you might want to have two hoops set up or have half the class doing something else. If the group is too large, then everyone doesn't have a chance to help pass people through and some of the impact is lost.

DISCUSSION IDEAS:
• What did you see happening during this activity?

- How were decisions made?
- Was everyone helping pass people through the hoop?
- Did everyone participate in the decision making process? Why or why not?
- Did any leaders emerge during this process? How did they emerge?
- Were all plans successful plans? Why were they tried?
- Did everyone agree with each plan that was tried? How was agreement or disagreement expressed in the group?
- Did the group ever stop and rethink what they were doing?
- Were you more successful or less successful after one of these regrouping sessions? Why?
- How can we apply this activity to group decisions you and your friends make?
- Describe some situations where a decision must be made by a group that you belong to.
- Why do you think that group decisions are harder to make than individual decisions?
- What were your feeling when the group would be sent back because someone touched the hoop or supports?
- How did you feel after you had been sent back repeatedly to try again?
- When people face this kind of frustration in life, what are some of the behaviors we see them doing?
- Did the group tend to blame the person who was being passed through, the person who touched or the group as a whole for poor planning? Why?
- How much control over his actions did the person who was being passed through have?
- What was the involvement of everyone in the group? Did some help pass, some support, some give

encouragement, some give advice, some just sit and watch?

- Was anyone afraid that they would be dropped? Why?
- How can you apply this activity to the real world?
- Describe some situations where individuals have relied upon others to help them through a problem.
- In groups are there some people who work harder and are more involved than others? Explain.
- How do you feel when you are in a group and there is a job to be done yet only some people are working hard?

PRESSURE POINT

TOPIC AREAS: Peer Pressure

CONCEPT: There is a difference between peer pressure that is long term and peer pressure that is short term. When you encounter a situation that you know is dangerous, harmful or illegal the best course of action is to remove yourself from the situation. The longer that you expose yourself to the situation, the harder it is to continue to refuse. An example would be going to a party and when you walk in; you discover that alcohol is being consumed. If you turn around and walk out, you will not have a hard time saying "no". If on the other hand you stay at the party with the good intention of not drinking, the pressure to drink will mount and be harder for you to resist. The moral of the story is to remove yourself from situations where you can encounter strong peer pressure to do something you feel is wrong.

METHOD: Classroom Activity

TIME FRAME: 10 Minutes plus discussion time

MATERIALS NEEDED:
- One wooden clothespin for each of the students in your class.
- A watch with a second hand on it.

ACTIVITY: Give each student in the class a clothespin. Tell them to hold the clothespin between their thumb and index finger. Have them use the hand that they do not write with. The clothespin should be held so that it is pointing away from the index finger and thumb in a direct line with the finger and the thumb. Just the tip of the finger and the tip of the thumb should be holding onto the clothespin. They are to hold the clothespin away from the body and not use any other part of their body to help with the activity.

Now, have them open and close the clothespin as many times as they can during a sixty second time period. You can keep track to see who can do this the most times. Now have them open the clothespin and keep it held open. The object being to see who can hold their clothespin open for the longest period of time. What you will find is that their fingers, hand and arm start to hurt after a period of time. Read the time out loud as they are doing this activity. It is best done with the kids standing up. When they can no longer hold their clothespin open, then they are to sit back down in their seats.

DISCUSSION IDEAS:
- How did you feel when you opened and closed the clothespin for sixty seconds?
- How much pain did you feel in your hand and arm?
- How did you feel when you had to hold the clothespin open for as long as possible?
- How much pain did you feel in your hand and arm?
- Did everyone sit down at the same time? Why not?
- Could you have held on for a longer period of time if you practiced a few times?
- How many of you still feel pain in your arm?
- List situations where this type of peer pressure problem might occur.

To relate this to peer pressure talk about the fact that when you first enter a questionable situation you need to remove yourself from it. That is demonstrated by the opening and closing of the clothespin which doesn't cause the same pain as holding the clothespin open. Holding it open shows how it is much harder and more painful to stay in a questionable situation and try to resist the pressure to engage in an activity that might be harmful. Point out to them that people did not sit down at the same rate. It is true that some people can resist pressure better than others. Also point out that with practice you can hold out against pressure for a longer period of time, but even with practice you might still give in at some point. The bottom line is to say "no" to the pressure and remove yourself from the situation.

QUICK DRAW

TOPIC AREAS: Communication, Values

CONCEPT: There are more ways to communicate than just talking and writing. This activity will explore one of those ways . . . pictures. It will give the kids a chance to get their message across in a fun yet challenging manner that requires them to go outside of their normal means of communicating. It also can be used to discuss values. The whole issue of cheating and winning without effort can be brought out into the open with this activity.

METHOD: Classroom Activity

TIME FRAME: 15 to 20 minutes plus discussion time

MATERIALS NEEDED:
- One felt tipped marker for every four or five people
- One 8½ by 11 piece of blank paper for every four or five people. You will need a new piece of paper for every two rounds that you play.
- A list of words for them to draw

ACTIVITY: Divide your class up into groups of four or five people. Each group will need a felt tip marker and a piece of blank paper. Spread the group out around the room. I like to have them work right on the floor, but tables would work too. Situate yourself in the middle of the room. You will have a list of six to seven words in each round that you would like for each group to draw. The activity is a lot like Pictionary except when a team gets a word right, they aren't done. After correctly guessing the word in your group you send the next drawer up to the leader, they whisper to the leader the word they just guessed, get the next word to draw whispered to them and the game continues. The first team done with the entire list of six or seven words is the winner of that round.

Let's see how that works: You call the first drawer up from each group and whisper the word for them to draw to all of them at one time. When you say start, they rush back to their respective groups and start drawing. Remind them that they can't use any letters or numbers in your drawing. When someone in their group guesses the correct word, another member of the group rushes up to the leader and whispers their guess in the leader's ear. If they are right, then the leader whispers the next word to them and off they go to draw. This continues until all groups have finished the entire list of words. Do not stop the round until all the groups have finished. You want everyone to experience the drawing part of the activity. You really do not care who finishes first, second and third.

A few helpful hints: Make sure the groups set up a rotation of drawers. Everyone on the team needs to take their turn drawing. Tell them they only get one piece of paper for every two complete rounds of words so use it carefully; that is part of the challenge. Warn them that they will play more than one round so they don't use up all of their paper in the first round. Stop the play after each round so teams may catch up and get even with everyone. Time will dictate how many rounds you play. Really emphasize no cheating. Since so much of the game is played in their individual groups it would be really easy to just go back to your circle and say the word quietly or mouth it to the other members.

Sample words you can use: Rocket, submarine, snowman, snowflake, garden, comb, coffee pot, sword, eraser, belt, windmill, microwave, etc.

DISCUSSION IDEAS:
- How did your group do in this activity?
- What was the hardest part of the activity?
- What problems did limited drawing space create for your group?
- How did you feel when you were the person doing the drawing?
- How did you feel when you were the person doing the guessing?
- What can this activity teach us about communicating?
- What is so hard about communicating through drawing?
- What are some other ways we communicate other than talking, writing and drawing?
- Did your group want to cheat?
- What made your group not cheat?
- How would you feel about winning if you knew you had cheated?
- How would you feel if you were beaten by a team you heard cheating?
- If there was a big prize for the winner, would that make a difference to you regarding your decision not to cheat?
- What are some of the situations you can think of where cheating would have been very helpful to you? Did you cheat or not? Why?
- How do you feel towards other people who cheat?
- What can this activity teach us about cheating?

QUIET LINE UP

TOPIC AREA: Communication

CONCEPT: We talk a lot about using something other than our voice to help us when we communicate. This activity will require the group to think about alternatives to talking when they communicate.

METHOD: Classroom Activity

TIME FRAME: 10 to 15 minutes plus discussion

MATERIALS NEEDED: None

ACTIVITY: Tell the group that the object of this activity is to form a single file line with the person whose birthday is closest to January 1st in the front and the person closest to December 31st in the back and everyone else in birthday order in between. There is a handicap. No one may not talk during the activity. They may use any method of communicating among themselves except for the mouthing of words. Give the group sixty seconds to talk among themselves to discuss various means of communicating without using their mouths before calling for silence. During this sixty seconds, they may not discuss birthdates. If you want the activity to be harder, do not give them any time to formulate communication alternatives.

DISCUSSION IDEAS:
- How did you feel when I first explained the activity?
- What made the activity difficult to accomplish?

- Did any leaders emerge during the activity? How were they chosen?
- What were some of the ways you used to communicate?
- What were some of the problems with this type of communication?
- What can this activity teach us about communication?
- List some of the methods of communication that could have been used in addition to those that were used.
- List ways in which we communicate with each other that do not involve talking?
- Are some methods are more effective than others? Why?

SLOWED REACTIONS

TOPIC AREAS: Alcohol, Other Drugs

CONCEPT: When you are under the influence of certain drugs your reactions will slow down and become impaired. Alcohol is a perfect example. It is a depressant and slows the body's reaction time down. This is evident when a person is driving under the influence. He will take much longer to react to an emergency situation than he would if he were sober. This longer reaction time is responsible for many of the automobile accidents on our highways today.

METHOD: Classroom Activity

TIME FRAME: 5 minutes plus discussion time

MATERIALS NEEDED: None

ACTIVITY: Have your group pair up in partners. Between the two partners, have them decide which one has the smaller shoe size. If both are identical then choose the person with the darkest hair color. This person is the leader. Have the other person put both of his arms straight out in front of him with the palms facing each other. Now have him cross his arms over each other with his arms still out straight. Now turn the palms so they face each other again and interlock the fingers. Then pull the hands in towards the body by going in a downward motion and then bring them up under his chin. Tell the leader that he is to ask the other person to move different fingers. The way he is to do this is to quickly point to a finger and say "Move this one", but do not touch the finger that he wants moved. Have them keep pointing to different fingers they want moved without too much time in between requests. Now have the partners switch roles and repeat the process. Most people will find that it is hard to move the correct finger.

Now have them repeat the entire activity but this time instead of just pointing to the finger that they want their partner to move, they are to touch the finger they want moved. Have them switch roles so both of the partners have this experience. Most people will find this is easier than the first activity was. In the first activity the brain could not figure out which finger it should move. By crossing the arms over and then pulling the hands up under the chin, you have confused the brain. Remember the brain is wired with the right side of the brain controlling the left side of the body and the left side of the brain controlling the right side of the body. When you cross your hands, your eyes cannot quickly tell the brain which finger to move. However, when the person touches the finger that he wants moved the brain has no problem. Now it doesn't have to rely on sight to tell it what to do, but now the brain has the sense of touch to give it a clue.

DISCUSSION IDEAS:
- What happened when your partner pointed to your fingers?
- What happened when your partner touched your fingers?
- Which activity was easier? Why?
- What can this activity tell us about being under the influence?

- If you are driving, what could happen during the time that it takes your brain to respond with the correct action?
- What other activities could be impaired by slowed reaction time?
- What kinds of jobs would be directly impacted if the person performing that job were under the influence?

SPEED

CONCEPT: When your body is under the influence of one of the drugs that speeds up your nervous system, you have less control over your actions. Your central nervous system is in high gear, but the messages that it receives are not reacted upon in the normal fashion. Even though the brain thinks it is doing a great job, in actuality performance is impaired.

METHOD: Classroom Activity

TIME FRAME: 10 minutes plus discussion time

MATERIALS NEEDED:
- A towel, a cone, or some other marker that can be moved

ACTIVITY: Have your group stand and form a circle. Have them hold hands. You will give them commands that they will need to follow. While still holding hands have them run in a circle. See how fast they can make one, two or three revolutions. Designate a leader of the circle. Now have them run and after they get up to speed, you place the marker on the ground. When the leader gets to the marker he is to stop. Everyone else in line is to stop as soon as the leader does. During the activity you can have them run clockwise and counter-clockwise. Always holding hands, have them run fast and slow. Sometimes have the marker placed way ahead of the leader and other times throw it down right in front of him. Change the leader often. What you should be seeing is that when the speed is fast or the marker is placed down only a short distance in front of the leader, then he is able to stop but the rest of the line has trouble stopping. At a slower speed this does not seem to be such a great problem. This has a direct correlation to the body under the influence of an "upper" or "speed". The mind can see what should be done, but the body can't react as it should because the central nervous system is actually over reacting.

DISCUSSION IDEAS:
- What was happening during this activity?
- How did it feel when you were the leader?
- How did it feel when you were not the leader?
- Could you stop easily when you were the leader?
- Could you stop easily when you were not the leader?
- What difference did your position relative to the leader have on your ability to stop?
- Did the speed of the group impact the ability of people to stop?
- What can this activity tell us about a body under the influence of a "speed" drug?
- What kinds of activities would be impaired by the use of "speed"?
- What kinds of jobs would be dangerous under the influence of "speed"?

SPIN AND PERFORM

TOPIC AREA: Alcohol

CONCEPT: When under the influence of alcohol, you body reacts in various ways. One reaction is that you can't control your movements with as much dexterity as you can when you are sober. This activity will show the loss of muscular control that you experience when under the influence of alcohol.

METHOD: Classroom Demonstration

TIME FRAME: 5 minutes plus discussion time

MATERIALS NEEDED:
- A pencil and paper or a piece of chalk and the blackboard
- A pitcher of water, a glass and a towel

ACTIVITY: Bring one student up in front of the class. Have him write his name on the blackboard or on a piece of paper. This is to establish his ability when he is sober. Now to simulate having him under the influence, spin him around until he is dizzy. When you stop him, immediately have him repeat writing his name. The attempt will not be anywhere near what it was before in either speed or clarity.

VARIATION:
A second method is to once again have one student up in front of the class. Have him pour water from a pitcher into a glass. Both the pitcher and the glass are

to be held in his hands. Now put the pitcher and glass down and spin him to get him dizzy. Immediately upon stopping, hand him the glass and pitcher and have him pour the water in the glass. He will probably spill some, so be sure a towel or something is under the glass.

DISCUSSIONS IDEAS:

- How did you feel when you wrote your name the first time?
- How did you feel when you tried to write your name after becoming dizzy?
- How did you feel when you poured the water the first time?
- How did you feel when you tried to pour the water after becoming dizzy?
- What were the signs that we saw showing that the student was impaired?
- What can these two activities show us about being under the influence?
- Would you want to ride in the car with either of these two people if they were driving? Why not?
- What kinds of activities that you participate in would be hampered if you participated in them while under the influence? Why?
- What kinds of jobs would be impossible to perform while under the influence?
- How drunk would a person have to be before you wouldn't let him drive the car you were riding in? Fly the plane you were flying in?

SQUEEZE

TOPIC AREAS: Tobacco, Other Drugs

CONCEPT: When nicotine enters the body system it constricts the blood vessels. This causes the blood to flow through a narrower opening. This elevates the body's blood pressure and causes the heart to work harder. Nicotine may enter the body through the smoking or chewing of tobacco. So switching from cigarettes to chewing tobacco is not a healthy solution. Other drugs such as "speed", also constrict the blood vessels and cause the same effects.

METHOD: Classroom Activity

TIME FRAME: 15 minutes plus discussion time

MATERIALS NEEDED:
• A rope long enough to go around all of the students in your class when they are standing in a group. The length will be about 35 feet for a group of thirty.

ACTIVITY: Have your students stand in a group in the middle of the room. Do not have them squeeze in close together. Take a rope and lay it on the ground so that it goes completely around the group and forms a circle. Now have all of the students step back out of the circle. Explain to them that you will be making the circle smaller and smaller. Each time you move the rope and make the circle smaller, it is their job to still get the entire class into the circle. They must have each person in the circle and no part of anyone's body may be touching the ground outside of the circle. Stress to the class that all movements must be done safely. No one is to jump or push their way into the circle. This rule is very important. Take some time to stress safety.

After a few rounds of making the circle smaller, they will have exhausted the easy solutions to the problem. No longer will it work to just squeeze in tighter. It is at this point that you may have to mention that they need to start working together and help each other if they are to continue being successful. At some point the circle will become too small for them to fit the entire class into. Don't let them quit too early; they are capable of more than they think they are. Do not give them too many suggestions or it will take the impact of the exercise away.

DISCUSSION IDEAS:
* What was happening during this activity?
* Why was it getting harder for you to fit inside the circle?
* Could the same number of people fit in the circle when it became smaller?
* Was it more difficult for the entire class to fit in the circle when it became smaller?
* What were some of the techniques you used the first couple of times the circle became smaller to still fit inside?
* Why did these techniques stop working?
* What were some of the techniques you used after the circle became too small to easily fit into?
* How can we relate this activity to the constriction of the blood vessels when nicotine is introduced into the body?
* What other drugs cause the blood vessels to narrow?

- In what ways does the body have to work harder when the blood vessels become narrower?
- What happens to body parts when they have to work harder than normal?

STRAIGHT WALKING

TOPIC AREA: Alcohol

CONCEPT: When you put alcohol into your system there are physiological changes you have no control over. When you use alcohol, one such change is in the area of balance. No matter how hard you try, when you are under the influence of alcohol, you will not be able to physically perform the same activities that you could when there wasn't alcohol in your system. This activity is one of the tests that law enforcement officers will give to a driver that they feel is under the influence.

METHOD: Classroom Demonstration

TIME FRAME: 5 minutes plus discussion time

MATERIALS NEEDED:
* A straight line on the floor about fifteen feet long. If there is not a line on the floor, you may use masking tape to make the line.

ACTIVITY: Have one student come up to the front of the group. Explain that they are to walk as quickly as they can, but when they take each step their heel must touch the toe of the foot that is on the ground. When they get to the end of the line, they are to turn around and walk back. Demonstrate this to the student so that he will understand and the class will see what is to be done. Now have the student repeat what you have demonstrated. This will give you a baseline to compare how he performs when under the influence. Since we can't actually get him drunk, we will do the next best thing. We will get him dizzy. This effects the inner ear equilibrium in much the same way that alcohol does. So bring the student back to the start of the line and spin him around enough times that he is good and dizzy. Now point him in the right direction and have him repeat the activity just as he did before. You should walk along with him to be sure he doesn't fall or bump into something while in this dizzy state. As he walks the line, it will be obvious that he is not doing as well as he did the first time. To insure this, be sure that you spin him around enough times to make him really dizzy.

DISCUSSION IDEAS:
- How did the student do the first time we tried this activity?
- How did the student do the second time we tried this activity?
- What was the difference between the two activities?
- Ask the student how he felt during both activities.
- How do you think this would affect a person trying to drive a car?
- What are some of the other activities that a person couldn't do when he was under the influence?
- Would you want to ride in a car with a person who is under the influence?
- How would you say "no" if someone who had been drinking offered you a ride?

STRESS TEST

TOPIC AREA: Stress

CONCEPT: Everyone encounters stress in their life. We can't avoid stress so we need to learn how to handle it. Before we can learn how to handle it, we need to understand the nature of stress and to recognize what makes it such a problem.

METHOD: Classroom Demonstration

TIME FRAME: 5 minutes plus discussion time

MATERIALS NEEDED:
• 6 tennis balls

ACTIVITY: Have one student come up to the front of the room. Explain that you are going to toss the tennis balls to him one at a time and he is to catch them and hold onto them. Throw the balls to him slowly and give him a good chance to catch as many as he can. Now retrieve the tennis balls and explain that you are going to toss them to him again, but faster this time. Toss them quick enough that he has trouble catching most of them. Stop and explain that sometimes problems come at you slow enough you can handle them easily, and sometimes they come too fast for you to handle all of them at the same time. This shows how stress can build up in your life. Then take all of the tennis balls and toss them to him at once. He will not be able to catch very many of them. Now explain that sometimes it doesn't have to be a lot of little things that build too much stress in our lives. Sometimes it can be just one very large problem such as a death in the family, breaking up with a boyfriend/girlfriend, a divorce, moving into a new area or school, etc. When this major problem hits you, your stress level may go to the extreme immediately.

DISCUSSION IDEAS:
- How did the catcher do when the tennis balls came at him slowly, one at a time?
- How did the catcher do when the tennis balls came at him faster, one at a time?
- How did the catcher do when the tennis balls were all tossed to him at one time?
- What can this activity tell us about stress in our lives?
- Let's list the things that cause stress in our lives.
- What are some of the ways you handle stress in your life?
- Are there positive and negative ways to handle stress?
- What are the positive ways to handle stress?
- What are the negative ways to handle stress?
- Is stress always bad for us?
- What makes stress bad for us?
- What makes stress good for us?

TELEGRAPH

TOPIC AREA: Communication

CONCEPT: As we communicate with each other, the messages we send are sometimes misunderstood. We need to be sure that what others hear is really what we mean. We also need to be sure that we understand what we are talking about before we try to explain it to someone else. Sometimes we send unclear messages and then wonder why people don't react the way we want them to. On the other hand, sometimes we listen to people who are not in the best position to be telling us what to do. Communication is both the sending of messages and the receiving of messages; it takes both to be a good communicator.

METHOD: Classroom Activity

TIME FRAME: 20 to 30 minutes plus discussion time

MATERIALS NEEDED:
- A quarter (25 cents)
- One tennis ball

ACTIVITY: Divide your class into two teams. Have them sit on the floor "Indian" style in two rows, facing each other. (This can be done in chairs, but some of the effect is lost.) Have each team hold hands. (If this is too disruptive in your class, they may grab the arm of the person next to them, but some of the effect is lost.) Position yourself between the two teams and at one end so that both people at the end of the line can see your hands. At the other end of the line, place the tennis ball half way between the last two people.

The activity begins by having everyone (except the two people at your end of the line) bow their heads and close their eyes, keeping them closed until the message is well past them. Then you flip the quarter into the air or juggle it in your hands and then show it to the first two people in the line at the same time. If the quarter shows heads, then they are to squeeze the hand of the person next to them. When each person feels the squeeze, they pass the message on down the line. When the last person in the line feels the squeeze, he opens his eyes and grabs the tennis ball. The team that grabs the ball first wins a point. When a point is won, the teams rotate towards the person who is controlling the quarter with the first person in line going to the end with the tennis ball. . This rotation will allow every person on the team a chance to play all the positions.

If the quarter comes up tails, then no squeeze is to be sent. However, sometimes the first person will mis-read the quarter and send a false message. If the message goes all the way to the end of the line and the ball is grabbed, then that team loses a point. No rotation is made at this time. If the person who is at the head of the line sends a false message and makes a sound that would indicate he has made a mistake, they automatically lose a point even if the message doesn't reach all the way to the end of the line. Sometimes a message is started by someone in the middle of the line by accident. The same rules apply if the ball is grabbed without a proper message being sent.

If you feel you are rotating too often, you may have them win two points before they rotate. I would suggest you play the first round with one win per rotation and then a second round with two wins per rotation. I also suggest that you mix the teams up before you go through a second rotation. This helps keep the game from getting too competitive and allows the students to continue playing for the fun of it, rather than the competition. I like to keep score just because it gives them something to shoot for.

Discussion Ideas:
- How did you feel when you were the person at the head of the line?
- How did you feel when you were the person at the end of the line?
- How did you feel when you were one of the people in the middle?
- How do you think a person feels when they send a wrong message?
- Did anyone in the group feel picked on because they made a mistake?
- Was it difficult to tell if the quarter was heads or tails?
- What can this activity tell us about communication?
- Have you ever heard of someone telling something that they later found out was not true? Describe the situation.
- Have you ever heard a rumor that you found out later was not true? Describe the situation.
- What happens when a rumor is started?
- When a rumor starts, how easy is it to stop?
- What are some of the ways that messages can be misunderstood?
- How easy is it to clear up misunderstandings once they have occurred? Why?
- How can poor communication hurt a friendship or relationship?

THE PUSH IS ON

TOPIC AREAS: Peer Pressure, Values

CONCEPT: There are two aspects to this activity. The first is peer pressure. Most refusal skill formulas include getting away from the situation after you have given your reasons for not wanting to use. This is important. You may have a real strong resolve not to use or to engage in any other activity that would be illegal or harmful to you, but the truth is that the longer you stay in that environment the more likely you will be to give in. The second aspect is that if you do not have any strong convictions against the behavior that is being suggested, then you will be easily persuaded. Without any values to fall back on, an individual can be convinced quite easily to change his "no" to "yes" without too much pressure. This is why we need to give our youth as many reasons as possible to avoid harmful situations. We can help create the values that they will relay upon by the information we expose them to.

METHOD: Classroom Demonstration

TIME FRAME: 5 minutes plus discussion time

MATERIALS NEEDED:
- One quart size glass jar with a mouth on it that is slightly smaller than a hard boiled egg. (I have used Gatorade bottles, fruit juice bottles and milk bottles)
- A minimum of two peeled hard boiled eggs
- A match
- A half piece of notebook paper

ACTIVITY: Put the glass bottle and one peeled hard boiled egg on a table in the front of the room. Invite one of your students to come up and try to push the hard boiled egg into the glass bottle. (Have one or more students try to accomplish this task.) The mouth of the bottle needs to be small enough that this will not be possible without breaking the egg. Now take the half piece of paper and loosely roll it up. Hold the paper in a horizontal position and light one end with the match. Allow it to begin burning and then drop it down into the glass bottle. Immediately place a different peeled hard boiled egg on top of the glass jar. Be sure that the narrower end of the egg is pointed into the glass bottle. Almost immediately the egg will be sucked down into the bottle. Don't be alarmed if there is very little flame. Not much is needed to complete the demonstration. To get the egg out of the bottle, you can cut it with a knife and it will fall out.

What you have done is scientifically very simple. The burning paper has consumed all of the air inside the glass bottle thereby creating a vacuum. The air pressure pushing down on the outside of the egg forces it into the bottle. While your students could not push the peeled hard boiled egg into the bottle, the vacuum could pull it into the bottle. You can use this to talk about staying in a harmful situation too long and your resistance being down. You can also talk about someone whose values aren't strong enough to withstand harmful situations being easily persuaded to join in when maybe they really didn't want to.

DISCUSSION IDEAS:
* What did we see happening when the students tried to push the egg into the bottle?

- What did we see happening when flame was placed into the bottle?
- Why do you think the egg went into the bottle when flame was used and it wouldn't go in when we pushed on it?
- How can we relate this activity to peer pressure?
- Please describe some situations where it is hard to say no?
- Is is harder to say no the longer you are in a situation? Why or why not?
- How does leaving a situation help us resist peer pressure?
- What can you do to help yourself resist the pressure to try something that might be harmful to you?
- What are values?
- Where and how do we get our values?
- Are values important?
- How do values help you make decisions?
- Are values good or bad?
- Can our values be changed?
- How would a person's values be changed?

THREAD THE NEEDLE

TOPIC AREAS: Alcohol, Other Drugs

CONCEPT: When our body is under the influence of alcohol or other drugs, we can not perform the same activities with our body as when we are not impaired by drugs. Manual dexterity is one bodily function that diminishes quickly when under the influence. The area of fine motor skills is especially affected.

METHOD: Classroom Activity

TIME FRAME: 25 minutes plus discussion

MATERIALS NEEDED:
* One pair of gloves for every four people
* One needle with a large eye for every four people
* A two foot long strand of thread for each participant

ACTIVITY: Divide your class into groups of four. Give each group one needle and each student one length of thread. Explain that each person in the group will have to take turns threading the needle, then taking the thread out and pass the needle to the next person and have them repeat the process. Keep doing this until each person in the group has successfully accomplished this task. Have the groups compete against each other for speed. This increases the pressure and makes the job even harder.

After completion by all groups, pass out a pair of gloves to each group. Explain that this time you will be doing the activity while impaired. To simulate this impairment, each person will have to wear the gloves when it is their turn to thread the needle.

DISCUSSION IDEAS:

- How well did you thread the needle when you were not wearing the gloves?
- How well did you thread the needle when you were wearing the gloves?
- What difference did wearing the gloves make?
- Did the pressure of having to compete against others bother you?
- What do you think this activity can tell us about alcohol and other drug impairment?
- What activities would be hard for you to accomplish while impaired?
- What jobs would you have a hard time doing while impaired?
- If pressure bothered you in this activity, how do you think an impaired person would react to situations where pressure was involved?
- Did any of you feel frustrated during this activity?
- Do you think a person who is under the influence would become frustrated quicker or slower than the normal person?
- How might this frustration be shown?
- Do you think that acting out behavior such as fighting would happen more often for a person that was impaired by alcohol or drugs? Why or why not?

TRUST CIRCLE

TOPIC AREAS: Problem Solving, Self Esteem

CONCEPT: Each person plays a special role in this world. None of us are the same and if any one of us was missing, then someone's life would be affected. We have to realize our own contribution to the world around us before we can truly feel good about ourselves. Our life affects the lives of others and their lives affect us.

METHOD: Classroom Activity

TIME FRAME: 10 minutes plus discussion time

MATERIALS NEEDED: None

ACTIVITY: Have your group stand in a circle. Each person must hold hands and then move the circle back until everyone is about arms length away from each other. This activity is a trust activity that demands that everyone contributes or it will not work. Have the group count off by two's. Now, while holding hands tightly, all of the number ones will begin to lean into the circle while at the same time the number twos will begin to lean backwards out of the circle. Do this slowly so that everyone will have a chance to pick up pressure on their arms from the people on either side of them. If the entire circle leans at the same time, the pressure is spread throughout the circle and no one person feels much of the weight. Hold this position for a few seconds. Once you have accomplished this goal, begin to have the number ones lean back up and the number twos lean into the circle. This is a tremendous activity to show the strength that a group can have when they work together.

VARIATION:

If you want to contrast this activity with people who aren't working together, have two people try to hold one person between them as they lean in and out. They will find that the person is heavier than when they were in the circle. They will also find out that the person can't lean as far either direction with only two people holding them.

DISCUSSION IDEAS:

* How did you feel when I first explained the activity?
* How did you feel when you were leaning into the circle?
* How did you feel when you were leaning out of the circle?
* What would have happened if one person did not take their responsibilities seriously?
* What makes this activity work?
* Why was it easier when the entire circle was leaning than when you were just holding one person between you?
* What would have happened to the circle if one person had decided to leave just when the leaning began?
* How important was each person in this activity?
* Describe other situations where one person is important to a group.
* Describe a situation you have been in where others would be affected if you left the group or situation.
* How does this exercise relate to your family?

- What can this exercise tell us about our own impact on the groups that we belong to?
- What can this exercise tell us about working together?

UNKNOWN

TOPIC AREA: Drugs

CONCEPT: When you are dealing with drugs, there are so many variables that you really don't know what the reaction of your body will be. You may have a weak heart or some other internal defect that you don't even know about. Then there is the uncertainty of the drugs themselves. Since street drugs are not made to conform with any federal laws, you don't know what goes into them. There have been numerous reports of rat poison, talcum powder and other chemicals that have been used to cut or make a drug stretch farther in order to allow the drug dealers to make a larger profit. What you see is not always what you get, and there are no "truth in advertising" laws for the dealers to worry about.

METHOD: Classroom Demonstration

TIME FRAME: 8 minutes plus discussion time

MATERIALS NEEDED:
- 5 water glasses
- 1 tablespoon
- 3 tablespoons of talcum powder
- 3 tablespoons of baking soda
- 3 tablespoons of flour
- 3 tablespoons of powdered confectioners sugar
- 1 cup of vinegar

ACTIVITY: Before class put 3 tablespoons of each powder into 4 separate glasses. One type of powder per glass. Crush the powders up so they look as much alike as possible. Also before class, pour approximately eight ounces of vinegar into the fifth glass. You don't want anyone to see you do this or the mystery will be solved before you even begin. Begin the activity by showing all four powders to the class and ask them to decide which one will cause a chemical reaction when mixed with a liquid. Do not tell them what the liquid or powders are or in any way identify them other than to number them. Have the class vote by a raise of hands which powder they think looks the most likely to cause a chemical reaction. Keep a record of how many votes each glass of powder receives. One glass at a time, add a couple of ounces of vinegar to each of the four glasses. Arrange your glasses so you pour the vinegar into the glass with the baking soda in it last. When the vinegar and baking soda come into contact with each other, you will see a chemical reaction which will consist of a lot of foaming. Be sure that you have something under all of the glasses. This will protect the surface you are working on. The glass with the baking soda in it will cause the most reaction. The others will have minimal reaction. Take a look at the votes and see how well your class guessed which white powder was the one that would react.

DISCUSSION IDEAS:
- How similar did the four powders look?
- What happened when the vinegar was added to each of the four powders?
- What criteria did you use to determine which powder you voted for before we added the vinegar?

- Was your criteria very useful?
- Was the entire class any better at guessing the correct powder than you were?
- What can this activity tell us about knowing what is contained inside a drug?
- Should we take the word of someone who gives us an illegal drug as to how safe it is? Why or why not?
- What is the drug dealer's reason for putting additional materials into a drug?
- What would some of the reasons be that people could react differently to the same drug?
- Do we really know how each person will react before they try a drug?

VANISHING CIRCLE

TOPIC AREA: Goal Setting

CONCEPT: When you set a goal it takes a number of things to help you accomplish your goal. One of the things it takes is help from other people. When the circle is large, it is easy for you to fit inside. Many times the early stages of accomplishing a goal are easier than the later stages. As things get tougher you need to have other people help you. The techniques that were used to fit into the circle as it became smaller demonstrate that we need help from others to accomplish our goals. You should also look at the concept of giving help to others to help them accomplish their goals.

METHOD: Classroom activity

TIME FRAME: 15 minutes plus discussion time

MATERIALS NEEDED:
- A rope long enough to go around all of the students in your class when they are standing in a group. The length will be about thirty five feet for a group of thirty.

ACTIVITY: Have your students stand in a group in the middle of the room. Do not have them squeeze in close together. Take a rope and lay it on the ground so that it goes completely around the group and forms a circle. Now have all of the students step back out of the circle. Explain to them that you will be making the circle smaller and smaller. Each time you move the rope and make the circle smaller, it is their job to still get the entire class into the circle. They must have each person in the circle and no one's foot or any other part of the body may be touching the ground outside of the circle. Stress to the class that all movements must be done safely. No one is to jump or push their way into the circle. This rule is very important. Take some time to stress safety.

After a few rounds of making the circle smaller, they will have exhausted the easy solutions to the problem. No longer will it work to just squeeze in tighter. It is at this point that you may have to mention that they need to start working together and help each other if they are to continue being successful. At some point the circle will become too small for them to fit the entire class into. Don't let them quit too early; they are capable of more than they think they are. Do not give them too many suggestions or it will take the impact of the exercise away.

DISCUSSION IDEAS:
- What was happening during this activity?
- Why was it harder for you to fit inside the circle?
- Was it more difficult for the entire class to fit inside the circle as it became smaller?
- What were some of the techniques you used in the beginning to fit inside?
- Why did these techniques stop working?
- What were some of the techniques that you used when the circle became smaller and smaller?
- How can we relate this activity to goal setting?
- What are some of the ways that we can help others to reach their goals?
- What are some of the ways that others can help us to reach our goals?
- When the solution looked impossible, how did you go about creating a solution?

WHOSE FAULT IS IT?

TOPIC AREAS: Decision Making, Peer Pressure

CONCEPT: When you allow yourself to be in situations where trouble can happen, the chances of it happening are much greater. If you want to avoid peer pressure, then you need to remove yourself from potentially dangerous situations. This is actually part of decision making. You need to consider all of the consequences to each decision that you make. There are always other people or events that can be blamed, but ultimately you have to take responsibility for your own actions no matter what the circumstances.

METHOD: Classroom Activity

TIME FRAME: 15 minutes plus discussion time

MATERIALS NEEDED:
• A copy of the story "It's Party Time" for each person

ACTIVITY: Divide your group into teams of four or five. Have them read the story out loud in each individual group. Then have each group rank the characters in the story from least responsible for Maria smoking the joint to the person most responsible for her smoking the joint. Everyone in the group must agree upon the ranking. Each group should be ready to verbally defend their ranking. After the groups are done with the assignment, have each group read out their ranked list and give their reasoning for the first two listings and the last listing. If you have the time, it is beneficial to have each group write their rankings on the blackboard or large tablet paper so that the different groups can visually compare the lists.

DISCUSSION IDEAS:
- How easy was it to get everyone to agree on the ranking?
- What method did you use to get agreement in the group?
- What criteria did you use to arrive at your ranking?
- What were the main facts from the story that influenced you in your ranking?
- What role did Mark play in Maria's use?
- What role did Mark's mom play in Maria's use?
- What role did Maria's parents play in Maria's use?
- What role did Shelly and Nicole play in Maria's use?
- What role did Hector play in Maria's use?
- What role did Maria play in her own use?
- At what points during the story could Maria have gotten out of the situation?
- What answers could she have used with her friends to say "no"?
- Mark only sold to his friends. Is he really a drug dealer?
- What circumstances led to Mark selling marijuana? Did these justify his being a drug dealer? Why or why not?
- Should Maria have been arrested as a drug user? Why or why not?
- Did Maria know what she was doing was wrong? Where in the story do you see that?
- What decisions did Maria make throughout the night that led to her using drugs?
- Describe situations that you or your friends have been in where things did not turn out exactly as you

thought they would because of decisions that were made.

- Have you ever had a friend who blames everything that happens to them on other people and events that they had no control over? How do you feel about them?
- Do other people have control over our actions? Explain

IT'S PARTY TIME

Mark is sitting at his bedroom desk rolling marijuana joints. He plans on selling them tonight at a big party he is having. His Mom is going out of town for the weekend and since his parents are divorced, he will have the house to himself. Ever since the divorce, money has been tight and Mark has found that selling pot is an easy way to make the money he needs for college. He is a senior and wants to attend the local university in the fall.

Unfortunately, Mark's bedroom door is slightly open and when his mom sticks her head in to say good-bye she spots the marijuana in front of him. She tells him to get rid of that stuff immediately. She doesn't want it in the house and tells him that it is dangerous and will fry his brain like an egg. Mark assures her that he will get rid of it and tells her not to worry because he never uses the stuff, he just sells it.

That night Maria came to the party with Hector and a couple of her girl friends, Shelly and Nicole. After they have been there about an hour, someone shouts "The keg's here!" and there is a mad rush for the kitchen. Maria doesn't drink. She thinks it tastes awful. As a matter of fact, she didn't even know that there was going to be booze at the party. Besides, her parents have said they would kill her if they ever catch her drinking or using drugs. However, Shelly and Nicole like to get a buzz so they keep after Maria to have at least one beer. Maria would like to go home, but Hector is so drunk he can't drive and she doesn't dare call her parents for fear they will find out she was at a beer bust.

Around midnight, Mark brings out the marijuana joints and offers them for sale around the room. Maria's friends pressure her to join them. To pressure her they ask, "What's the matter, are you too good for us?", "Come on, you wouldn't drink with us so the least you could do is join us in a smoke!", and "A real friend would give it a try!". Finally Maria gives in and goes with them out to the back porch where it is quieter. Just as Maria takes the joint and inhales, a spot light shines on the porch and they hear "Stand right where you are. This is the police and you are under arrest!".

Please rank the individuals in this story from the person most responsible for Maria having smoked the joint, to the person least responsible. Be ready to give reasons for your ranking.

Mark	Maria	Shelly and Nicole
Mark's mom	Maria's parents	Hector

BIBLIOGRAPHY AND RESOURCE LIST

Cooperation In The Classroom, David Johnson, Roger Johnson & Edythe Johnson Holubec, Interaction Book Co., Edina, Minnesota, 1991.

Cooperative Learning, Spencer Kagan PH.D., Resources for Teacher Inc., San Juan Capistrano, California, 1992.

Cooperation: Learning through Laughter, Charlene C. Wenc, The Americas Institute of Adlerian Studies, LTD., Chicago, Illinois, 1986.

Cowstails and Cobras II, Karl Rohnke, Kendall/Hunt Publishing Co., Dubuque, Iowa, 1989.

Creative Teaching Methods, Marlene D. LeFever, David C. Cook Publishing Co., Elgin, Illinois, 1985.

Do It! Active Learning In Youth Ministry, Thom & Joani Schultz, Group Books, Loveland, Colorado, 1989.

Experiential Education and the Schools, Richard Kraft & James Kielsmeier, Association for Experiential Education, Boulder, Colorado, 1986.

Games for Social and Life Skills, Tim Bond, Nichols Publishing Co., New York, 1986.

Games Trainers Play, John W. Newstrom & Edward E. Scannell, McGraw Hill Book Co., New York, N.Y., 1980.

Get'Em Talking, Mike Yaconelli and Scott Koenig-saecker, Zondervan Publishing House, Grand Rapids, Michigan, 1989.

How To Lead Small Groups, Neal McBride, NAV-PRESS, Colorado Springs, CO, 1984.

Islands of Healing, Jim Schoel, Dick Prouty & Paul

Rodcliff, Project Adventure Inc, Hamilton, Massachusetts, 1988.

Leadership Training Through Gaming, Elizabeth M. Christopher & Larry E. Smith, Nichols Publishing Co., New York, 1987.

More Games Trainers Play, John W. Newstrom & Edward E. Scannell, McGraw Hill Book Co., New York, N.Y., 1983.

New Games For the Whole Family, Dale N. LeFevre, Putnam Publishing Group, New York, N.Y., 1988.

Outrageous Object Lessons, E.G. Von Trutzschler, Gospel Light Publications, Ventura, California, 1987.

Peer Counseling, Judith A. Tindall Ph.D., Accelerated Development Inc., Muncie, Indiana, 1989.

Playfair, Matt Weinstein and Joel Goodman, Impact Publishers, San Luis Obispo, California, 1980.

Science Demonstrations for the Elementary Classroom, Dorothea Allen, Parker Publishing Co., West Nyack, N.Y., 1988

Silver Bullets, Karl Rohnke, Kendall/Hunt Publishing Co., Dubuque, Iowa, 1984.

Skills for Living, Rosemarie S. Morganett, Research Press, Champsign, Illinois, 1990.

Still More Games Trainers Play, John W. Newstrom & Edward E. Scannell, McGraw Hill Book Co., New York, N.Y., 1991.

Substance Abuse Prevention Activities for Elementary Students, Patricia J. Gerne & Timothy A. Gerne, Prentice Hall, Edgewood Cliffs, New Jersey, 1986.

Substance Abuse Prevention Activities of Secondary Students, Patricia J. Gerne & Timothy A. Gerne, Prentice Hall, Englewood Cliffs, New Jersey, 1991.

Teaching The Bible Creatively, Bill McNabb and Steven Mabry, Zondervan Publishing House, Grand Rapids, Michigan, 1984.

Teaching To Change Lives, Howard G. Hendricks, Mult-nomah, Portland, Oregan, 1987.

The Theory of Experiential Education, Richard Kraft & James Kielsmeier, Association for Experiential Education, Boulder, Colorado, 1986.

Thinking, Feeling, Behaving, Ann Vernon, Research Press, Champaign, Illinois, 1989.

Workplay, Carmine M. Consalvo, Organizational Design and Development Inc., King of Prussia, Pennsylvania, 1992.

TOPICAL INDEX

TOPIC AREA: Title of Activity, Page Number

ADDICTION:
All Tied Up, 62
Frogman, 127
In The Driver's Seat, 146

ADVERTISING:
Lights-Camera-Action, 153

ALCOHOL:
All Thumbs, 59
Bad Vision, 80
Balloon Race, 82
Circle Juggle, 106
Connections, 114
Dollar Bill Jump, 122
Group Sculpture, 132
In The Driver's Seat, 146
Liver Overload, 158
Slowed Reactions, 193
Spin and Perform, 198
Straight Walking, 203
Thread The Needle, 213

CLIQUES:
How Does It Feel?, 141
Left Out, 151

COMMUNICATION:
Awesome Lap Sit, 70
Back Art, 73
Back To Back Drawing, 76
Blind Walk, 87
Body Shuffle, 90
Building What You Hear, 96
Four On A String, 124
Group Sculpture, 132
How Bad Can You Be?, 139
Pass Right - Pass Left, 170

Quick Draw, 188
Quiet Line Up, 191
Telegraph, 207

DECISION MAKING:
Body Shuffle, 90
Bridges, 93
Choices and Consequences, 100
Mount Everest, 167
People Jump, 174
Porthole, 180
Whose Fault Is It?, 223

DRUGS:
A Million Dollars, 56
All Thumbs, 59
Balloon Race, 82
Circle Juggle, 106
Connections, 114
Dollar Bill Jump, 122
Group Sculpture, 132
In The Driver's Seat, 146
Slowed Reactions, 193
Speed, 196
Squeeze, 200
Thread The Needle, 213
Unknown, 218

GOAL SETTING
Auction Block, 64
Circle Juggle With A Goal, 110
Copy Cat, 117
I'll Bet You Can't, 144
Mind Power, 164
People Lift, 177
Vanishing Circle, 221
HABITS:
All Tied Up, 62

PEER PRESSURE:
Decide Early, 119
Gorilla Game, 129
I'll Bet You Can't, 144
Magic Cup, 160
Pressure Point, 185
The Push Is On, 210
Whose Fault Is It?, 223

PROBLEM SOLVING:
Awesome Lap Sit, 70
Body Shuffle, 90
Bridges, 93
Marshmallow Tower, 162
Mount Everest, 167
People Jump, 174
Porthole, 180
Trust Circle, 215

SELF ESTEEM:
Group Treasure Hunt, 135
Line Up, 156
Trust Circle, 215

STRESS:
Circle Juggle, 106
Stress Test, 205

TOBACCO:
Cilia Volleyball, 103
Jogging In Place, 149
Squeeze, 200

VALUES:
A Million Dollars, 56
Auction Block, 64
How Does It Feel?, 141
Quick Draw, 188
The Push Is On, 210

ACTIVITIES THAT TEACH WORKSHOP

- Bring this full day, half day, or evening workshop to your area.

- Experience for yourself these activities in a hands-on workshop.

- See the Active Learning Model in action.

- Learn the helpful hints that are too difficult to convey in a book.

- Workshop will be lead by book's author, Tom Jackson.

Call or write for more information!

Tom Jackson
3835 West 800 North
Cedar City UT 84720

(435) 586-7058

Additional copies of this book may be ordered from the address listed above.